# GOD'S LAUGHTER

Marianne Dubois

# GOD'S LAUGHTER

*or*

# Giving Birth to Joy

*English translation by*
Deborah Honoré

First published in 1994 French as Le Rire de Dieu by Editions Dervy
English translation published in 2000 by
Hazelwood Press
Loddiswell,
Nr. Kingsbridge TQ7 4EB



By the same author:

*Solar Encounters*

published by
Hazelwood Press



ISBN 1-901272-31-1
(French edition ISBN 2-85076-627-5
Publisher DERVY Paris)

Printed and bound by Parchment (Oxford) Limited
Printworks, Crescent Road,
Cowley, Oxford OX4 2PB

# Table of Contents

# FOREWORD

The title *God's Laughter* sets the tone for the questions and answers found in this book. Its aim is simply to open the imagination to splendour, to dazzling joy, to poetry, to creation and to love.

The image of the divine that has sprung to life in me is increasingly a laughing presence.

If a face forms in my inner space, its expression is tenderly teasing. It is often lit by unpredictable laughter: laughter gathering secretly round the eyes before bursting through like a great wave of relief that transforms everything in its path.

By taking the name of Jesus, this image places itself within a tradition.

I am well aware that a laughing Jesus is not easy to accept. Nonetheless it is his laughter that is alive in every cell and in which I exult.

In addition, the title relates to the questions because the spirit of freedom breathes through the answers, and

God's Laughter expresses this freedom.

Laughter can flow through every instant of our lives even when circumstances are very serious. If it comes from our roots it transcends our troubles, and instantly shows up what is absurd both in the situation and in the behaviour that provoked it.

In these troubled times when mutations are multiplying and many people lock themselves into fear and distrust, the laughter of freedom daily becomes more essential.

Can you imagine any more joyful, or more spectacular "fireworks", than God's Laughter? It is the laughter of rivers flowing in gentle valleys, of dawn breaking on the first morning of the universe.

And it is hullabaloo, it is music, it is also the madness of loving.

It sweeps one off, lights everything up and brings delight.

It breaks down our boundaries.

May God's Laughter show us the way to our true selves, at the heart of those invisible lands where joy perpetuates itself without ever being exhausted.

# PREFACE

To introduce this work, I need to give an account of the experience, or rather the "spiritual adventure", I have been living with such intensity. This is the origin of its unfolding.

The first changes came about after a bereavement or in fact shortly before, when one sees painfully that the person with whom one has shared one's life is going to die.

The death of my life's companion was very hard to bear. However it was at this time that a veil was lifted for me.

I had begun to be aware from a distance not only of his condition while he was in intensive care, but also to hear some of his calls for help. I was not with him in the hospital at the moment of his death—I was at home but sensed he was dying.

I felt I was being plunged into a different state of consciousness and I let myself be guided by an inner impulse.

On this plane I was wholly at his side and accompanied him in the passage from life to death.

Words came to me: "Go further—leave your body—go higher—you are going towards the light—I love you—don't be afraid—those grimacing faces round you are only reflections of your anxiety".

After some time, I don't know how long, an incredible, indescribable light flooded us both.

I heard myself say "It is wonderful".

A few moments later, they rang from the hospital to tell me that he had died.

It seems that this event had a bearing on what has followed, but I cannot be absolutely sure.

About six months later, I was led to "live" inwardly my first encounter with Jesus.

This did not take place in everyday reality but in another reality that feels far more alive and intense than the everyday plane.

In this "inner vision" I am at home in the country, alone and sad. It is winter. It is late and I am surprised to hear the doorbell ring. I am a little afraid ...

I go downstairs and see a shaft of light coming from under the front door. How is this possible when there is no lighting in the street? I wonder if I am going mad, but nevertheless walk up to the door. With a pounding heart, I wait a few moments, then fling it open...

Jesus is there in front of me. Astounded, I look at this apparition, whose white, still outline I recognise at once.

Why Jesus? I had no premonition as yet of the incredible love story that would turn my life upside down. Christianity had no place in my conscious mind. The inwardly serene images of the Buddha, or the Chinese wisdom of Lao Tse had appealed to me more.

In seeing Jesus at my door, I think he hasn't come to me, he's made a mistake. I sink down at his feet and in my heart ask him to go.

That is when he takes my hands, lifts me up and comes into my house.

At this point it is no longer a matter of anecdote but becomes a real upheaval of the soul, something that cannot be communicated.

His compassion is infinite; it floods into me like a torrent, overturning everything in its path. I surrender to it and weep till drained of all the tears that have been refused since the beginning of the world.

How can one accept this love, a love so great that it asks for nothing?

*"I am your Source, I am yourself"* are his first words to me.

This is how my heart has filled with light and my grey and anxious life has begun to open itself to the great sun of fulfilment.

Some weeks later another "inner apparition" occurred, this time very different, then another... Then the encounters followed closer and closer on each other until this presence became an almost constant part of me with which I could converse.

Each thought, each action, each mundane problem is now recast and transformed in the look of this presence, as if it was me but at a different level of awareness. I now "see" myself ever more accurately and keenly. I entrust him with every moment of my life in the clearest and truest perception I can offer. This calls for courage and attention, but it seems that strength is growing and propels me towards my other self.

A series of encounters and dialogues with this "image of Love" has not only transformed my everyday life, but also the way I look at the world, my way of being and thinking. My body feels different. It is as if each cell were coming to life, developing an awareness of itself together with a global awareness. But how can one describe a body which "tests" existence by becoming limitless? My only way is to use images and I do not know to what extent they can convey this different level of reality where body, mind and soul are no longer separate.

After a time, I noticed that, when I let myself go completely into a certain state of relaxation and openness, the part of me which is connected could "speak". Then the answers to questions do not come from my ego, but reflect what is obscurely sensed in the questioner's own depths.

In living this experience, I am in no way an intermediary or medium because I myself, with my essential being, am wholly involved in the answers that are given. Only they have nothing whatever to do with my ego.

These answers, like my other writings, cannot be transmitted unless I am the living evidence of their contents. It is the necessary condition of their accuracy. Unity exists where I am my true self and not an intermediary receiving something other than my most essentially lived reality.

It seems that for me the possibility of answering requests is a creative process analogous to an artist's inspiration, but an artist whose work is in no way separate from ordinary life, from everyday thoughts or actions.

I am nobody's letterbox, neither am I a telephone for some unknown in the beyond—unless nothing separates the box from the letters it receives, or the telephone from the messages it transmits.

This experience represents a crucial transformation of being.

All the points of reference stored up during my life have had to be abandoned. I find myself on a ship bound for the unknown with an invisible guide who fills the universe as he fills me. My name for him is Jesus, but I have since realized that all names suit him, for the divine can burst through every name and all forms.

For those who can't envisage giving him personality or a name, he is the "Nameless" or the "Unimaginable".

For practical ease and because it is my most beautiful, my dearest and tenderest image of love, the answers come from this source. It is "HE" who answers through me, or if one prefers it, the answer comes from a deeper part of myself. "HE", therefore, is Jesus, but a Jesus of every imaginable colour who cannot be fitted into any structure because he has no limits. "HE" in each one of us is the bit that is free and connected. In everything, "HE" is the infinite source. In meeting him, I felt I was meeting myself at last and merging with the unity of life.

In this unity joy is immeasurable and death inconceivable. Outwardly nothing seems to have changed, but fear, duty and guilt are replaced by the unbelievable happiness of swimming with the current of a different reality. In this reality it is as if my body itself is evolving. For one thing, vital energy develops differently and frees new circuits; for another, consciously welcoming this "image" appears to transform the substance of my being.

"*Love alone transforms your cells*" is a phrase that often appears. Without a doubt it is the keystone.

Later I understood why it was Jesus' image that appeared rather than any other: this image of Love has been at work in the western unconscious mind for nearly two thousand years. Perhaps the time has come for another birth, for a "resurrection" in the heart of each person, to free his image from the jumble of dogmas and from every sort of religious constraint. Love is One. Nothing divides it, even if thousands of paths lead us to it.

In the course of this experience a dialogue has been established between the everyday me and my deepest self. This dialogue has continued uninterrupted now for over eight years and it is in this way that "HE" or Jesus, the infinite fountain of Love, answers our questions.

In *God's Laughter* the questions are asked by readers, by friends or by people during talks. Many also are my own questions. Answers come either orally or by being written. Sometimes they are written down after having been given orally.

This "adventure" or transformation of the body, soul and mind continues to follow its unpredictable course, but is always accompanied by the great warmth and freedom of laughter, in open and boundless joy.

# INTRODUCTION

The questions and answers found here deal with a wide range of life's problems. They can concern relationships, be personal or general, psychological, ethical, existential, or spiritual, and seem to result from a need that is peculiar to our times. The answers are not wholly adjusted to every person, for they take account of the deep beliefs of the questioner, but almost always there is something in them that speaks to each one of us. Usually they are addressed to someone specific and reflect a secret part of that person, but sometimes they are addressed to everyone on earth.

Through the answer that comes for them, each one can find a more intimate relationship with himself or herself; but others, too, can find that the answer speaks to them and through these texts discover a door that opens, a landscape that is illumined or a lost key.

The answers seem to come from a shore that we all share, a place where we are all connected.

The messages therefore are adapted to the beliefs each one of us holds. If you have a special relationship with Jesus, then obviously it is Jesus who gives you his Love, his understanding and total acceptance of what you are. If you are an atheist, you will be spoken to in the name of life. If you have a master either living or from the past, or indeed any kind of image of the divine, the answers will come to you from that source. Belief in reincarnation will be taken into account as much as nonbelief. If you have an abstract perception of unity, you will be answered according to that perception. Wherever we stand, each one of us is accompanied by the unconditional love that makes possible a few steps towards joy, as well as greater acceptance of oneself and others.

Whenever some truth is considered to be absolute it leads people in one way or another to destroy or despise those who do not conform to their concept.

Because we are limited, however, any absolute truth is inconceivable for us. The only thing that matters is to go fully into one's own inner and personal truth, the truth corresponding most nearly to what we are at that moment.

These texts could allow us, according to our capacities, to come closer to the small spark of truth for which each one of us is responsible. This would enable us to understand the spark in other people and to aim at widening our field of awareness, perhaps even at a true transformation.

***Question:*** At what level of consciousness can one interpret the answers given in these writings?

***He says:*** On the level of the absolute, there is no problem: life has neither beginning nor end. No questions have meaning except to confirm the illusion that we have of ourselves. From this point of view, even the disappearance of the earth would have no reality. But the following chapters refer to the immediate world of duality. It is through sorting out our daily problems that we may perhaps get closer to another level of consciousness.

It is suggested nevertheless that in everyday life we transcend the dualistic attitude we have always been taught. For example, it is proposed that we give vent to feelings of rebellion, fear, suffering, repressed violence, sexual difficulties, etc., and live them out to their fullest extent, but in ourselves. There is no question here of letting go and expressing them in actual reality. What is involved is "seeing" the emotion and accepting it for what it is without judging it. Through understanding and non-judgement these unwanted or troubling urges can dissolve in the unity. Repression merely strengthens or perverts them, or else makes one ill.

The way to resolve the problem lies in the mental images that convey the emotion, obviously not in actions which could do harm, or in negative thoughts about others or oneself.

As an example, instead of repressing one's anger at someone, notice the mental images which present themselves—one would like to strangle him—look at this urge—other images appear—look at them, and so on until the anger is totally exhausted.

This neutral observation leads to transformation. Observation stripped of all judgement and so of all guilt allows the emotion to run dry. There is no question of hurting anyone at any level. It is a process that relates only to the negative image that has built up. One can transform it by taking one's anger with someone to its furthest point, accepting it wholly, withholding none of it. In this way one can work right through this negative emotion. One is then freed from one's image of that person and release can take place. On a different plane of consciousness, the other person also feels released from the grip of that projected anger.

But to see clearly calls for an attentiveness that seems particularly difficult to most of us. It is, however, the foundation of all inner research and of the happiness that comes from it. Lack of clarity may perhaps protect us to a certain extent from the "unknown" that we are to ourselves, but it separates us for ever from the least bit of true inner freedom.

## Chapter One

# Emotional Life

***Question:*** *My daughter hasn't found her path in life. She throws herself into all sorts of activities that society condemns. I think I have failed to bring her up properly and feel ashamed. What should I do?*

***He says:*** Your daughter is a flaming banner giving you courage to become yourself. She leads you into areas that you would never have dreamed of.

Look at her differently, see her as a torch that brings you light. She teaches you love, of the sort that doesn't conform to a model. Wipe out of your heart the image of your child that society reflects to you through its idiotic judgements. Dare to live unaffected by other people's conventions. Your child is there to help you get over shame and be proud of what you are, in the dazzling splendour of new-found freedom. She is urging you to shake off the burdens other impose on you. Let laughter fill you as you shed everything that isn't an essential part of yourself. Find this essential part again, now hidden behind the screen of a suffocating education, an education that turned you into a much too well-behaved little girl. Your child lets you recover the life blood of rebellion you have always stifled. Rebellion that demands to be set free, looked at, and brought fully to light. It is this that can save you and save your child. Don't let it rot away, behind walls erected out of fear and other people's opinions.

It is in accepting the truth of what you are that the answer to your problems lies, not in the repression brought to bear on either you or your daughter by those who believe they have to impose their rigid and loveless morals.

Tear every form of repression out of yourself, including what you yourself repress, and walk confidently towards the freedom that at last lets you spread your wings.

This is how to discover your strength and your riches and show others what you really are, because then each action and each word will come naturally from your deepest source. The gift of truth is what your child wants from you. This gift will be as liberating for her as it will be for you.

***Question:*** *How can I stop being dependent on drugs?*

***He says:*** Have you understood why you seek a refuge in drugs? What is your unhappiness, your despair, your disgust with living, and your refusal to accept the world and your existence as they are? Do you want to escape from yourself, or need to find sensations that give you access to other levels of reality? Or is it perhaps the fear of not measuring up to things that has taken away all your self-confidence?

If you stray into this kind of dependence, it shows that you are looking for something to transcend your everyday life because you find it boring, ugly or unbearable to live with.

Don't you hope to find the light that makes your path beautiful, the spark that transforms your life? Can you believe that the divine is actually in you and can guide you towards this light, without your having to destroy yourself?

To start with, understand very intimately what you want to compensate for, or what you are lacking and why you lack it. If you go right into this intrinsic sorrow, into this need to escape from everything that offends you, into the weakness that stops you from holding yourself proudly in life, whatever the circumstances; if you can be "one" with the deep cause of your dependence, you will be able to drop it.

It is a question of attention and non-judgement, for attention and non-judgement lead you to AWARENESS.

Observe the mechanism that leads you to destruction. Don't you find there some obscure wish to destroy yourself, or to revenge yourself for all that "they" have done to you?

Is it society, a parent, the family, pressure from a religious system or a narrow-minded morality that drives you more or less consciously to seek revenge, even if only against yourself?

Once you have understood your mechanism in its complexity, you will be able to ask for help, and if you sincerely desire it you will be able to free yourself from your dependence. Don't go on living in secrecy and shame. Real understanding leads you to an awareness that in itself is already a healing. It is the seed of your growth and if you can see and feel it as such, it will change your attitude to yourself and to the world. It will show you a new way of consciousness, in itself a working tool with which to rebuild your life and discover joy.

What could you do in practical terms to give up your dependence on drugs or anything else?

Each day when you get up, look at yourself with a fresh eye, with tenderness for yourself and all your weaknesses. Not with a view to indulging yourself, but from an angle of understanding and love. Think up some short phrase that would fit this and support you throughout the day. For example: "Happiness is hidden, if I find it, I shall have no need for drugs"— or else: "The divine look is protecting me whatever I do"— or again: "Life in me is more powerful than any addiction". You will find for yourself the short phrase that can help you and set the tone for your day. In this way every day you will be able to reach a new level, find new strength, and notice that you are walking calmly towards your freedom.

***Question:*** *Why has J. cried ever since his birth? (He is 3 months old.)*

***He says:*** For the moment, J. has no other way of expressing what is an explosive force, his life force. He needs a lot to distract him until he can manage things for himself. He feels shut in, imprisoned in too small a body which hasn't yet any way to express itself.

The coming generation for the most part is richly endowed and has a special gift for putting together and building a new world. It has great inner strength and will be a strong pillar for the future.

Parents are therefore called on to have patience, to love and support their child even if sometimes they are troubled by what takes place.

Our children will outstrip us beyond anything we can imagine, especially those of this generation.

At the moment J. is asking his mother to communicate with him at a very deep level. He is hungering for soul contact and feels himself trapped by the constraints of his small body. He wants to be spoken to with truth, not just with words, but with the warmth of heart and soul that goes beyond words. He wants his mother to go deeper than the usual guidelines associated with looking after a child. He is in contact with the part of her that is connected to the unity of life. J. is in this unity and does not understand why his mother isn't always there and why she doesn't share in the inordinate aspiration that fills him. If she can contact him in that further part of herself, the deep part that is not separated, she will understand her child's needs "viscerally". He will calm down straight away. There is no cause for anxiety. He is an outstanding child who needs to be accepted along with his cries of despair. Understanding will help him through this period of becoming adapted to an incarnation that for the moment he finds hard to accept.

***Question:*** *What is the difference between detachment and indifference? Isn't detachment heading for withdrawal and cutting oneself off? Has it any place in the education of children?*

***He says:*** With this sort of question it is essential to agree on the meaning one gives to words. The word detachment is often used in the sense of indifference. It is useful therefore to specify that here it is used as a negation of egotistic attachment. Then it is the opposite of indifference because when you are indifferent you cut yourself off from others, whereas in detachment you are with them but do not make any demands on them. You join them with the part of yourself that is not the ego. You sense them in you as a part of your own being, because you expect nothing of them. So the relationship is neutral, that is to say free, not involved in any exchange of power. The exchange of power puts chains on a relationship. For instance if you say to someone: I am doing this for your sake— but in fact implicitly and more or less consciously you oblige the other to go along with your demands in exchange for the service rendered—you are in a relation of power.

Another example: you project onto someone the wish that they should change, it would be for their own good, their happiness, etc. In wanting something from others, in the name of morals or a personal preference, you base your life, all in good faith, on blackmail.

If you are detached as we defined it, you accept others as they are, you can include them completely and carry them in your heart. Otherwise you sever the current that links you together at the secret level of being.

This is why children's education is so delicate a matter. How to avoid constraint and yet lead them towards a healthy adaptation to society and all that life inevitably has in store for them? The only answers lie in listening and attention combined with great flexibility. It is all about encouraging one's child to make the best of its abilities while allowing it to feel free within a reassuring structure. There, once again, unconditional love is the best guide.

A couple's harmony is the best legacy they can hand on to children. That is the chief factor in providing this reassuring structure.

If parents could be aware of the difference between the actual gifts of their child and the ambitions they have for it, many mistakes could be avoided.

By questioning yourself in every new situation, in other words by staying fully alive, you will inevitably move towards the "detachment" from the ego, or "non-identification", which is another form of love.

This form of love corresponds to the beating heart of the universe and excludes neither anything nor anyone, for it is the current of life itself.

***Question:*** *How can we help our son who no longer seems to enjoy studying the subjects he has chosen?*

***He says:*** J. needs to be accepted as he is, to be recognized for his own qualities, which are sensitivity, good taste, and an unusually intelligent heart. He is someone of exceptional quality whose desire to do well and whose vulnerability sometimes weigh him down. He wants to prove to himself and to others that he is capable of living up to their expectations, for as yet he is too young to see himself clearly. His choices are inevitably influenced by what his parents desire for him, even when that is unexpressed. He doesn't always feel equal to it, but having got caught up he doesn't want to back out even if he feels a sort of inner collapse.

Unconditional and dispassionate support could defuse the situation and help him to discover his own way. He would feel more comfortable if he had more time free from anxiety to mature and expand.

His great perceptiveness both of feeling and of his sense of being means that he is always ready to listen. Later on his artistic gifts combined with his other abilities will lead him into a profession where he will be able to make use of all his gifts and he will develop in a new direction.

At the moment he senses the anxiety of those he loves. It flows into his own and increases it. When he has found his own strength and way he will be part of the new humanity that can open itself to other levels of awareness. Each time one can offer him the neutral ground that leaves him free to discover his originality without feeding his anxiety, one helps him to find himself and head towards a transformation that won't be stopped.

***Question:*** *Why is there violence and despair among some adolescents?*

***He says:*** The skilful and constant emphasis on any negative event that the media orchestrates, is a subtle pollutant of the mind.

When does one ever hear about the great majority of

young people who are working with complete disinterest in humanitarian undertakings? This is an absolutely new phenomenon on earth. A growing sense of solidarity is finding its place. It is served by courage, efficiency and self-denial.

If the media would only lean a little further in this direction, they would do useful work in the minds of many people. Let us ignore the negative bludgeoning as much as we can. Violence and despair are the prerogative of a very small minority.

We won't speak here of those young murderers whose minds are clearly disturbed.

When an adolescent does sink into violence and despair, we need to understand that there is a great hole in the picture he has of himself and of his future. Very likely deprived of understanding and love, he has been subjected to a family that could give him no reason to exist. How can he not want to smash everything when it seems that the only idol worshipped in grown-up circles is the god of money, possessions, cars and all the rest? If his environment is underprivileged, it is precisely television that sets the example— violence, negativity, consumption. The family provides no compensation to redress the balance. Where can he find a way out, a little hope, a little dream?

We are all responsible for these unfortunate children. They are a part of ourselves. They reflect to us what we are, we who judge and very often know neither how to love nor how to share.

So it is not for us to feel guilty but to look clearly at our own lives in order to understand these young adolescents better.

***Question:*** *What is the origin of tiredness and how can one avoid it?*

***He says:*** If lack of sleep, illness or unsuitable physical work are not responsible, tiredness arises in the mind. It lies precisely in the area of projections linked to time. For instance: you are working so hard you must obviously be worn out. The thought relays the message to the subconscious and tiredness sets in. Or take another example: you project that you will never be able to cope. Immediately you are crushed by tiredness.

This state also stems from likes and dislikes. You are hardly ever tired if you do things with pleasure. When you dislike doing them, you tire very quickly. If you empty your head of these notions of constraint or dislike and stop shutting the idea of some prospective work into time and fixity, no tiredness can reach you. Turn your chores into discoveries, look at them differently. Look at them with a lively eye that transforms them. Your actions have no other importance for you than what you give them. Constraints build up in your thoughts; so act without preconceived ideas, and without locking your projects into rigid constructions. Don't take on engagements that overstrain your capacities. Stress is a nervous and exacerbated form of tiredness. A mechanism of breathlessness and permanent pressure starts up and the machine accelerates faster and faster, till it finally spins round onto itself for no reason. It is as if pressure had become the dominant factor in existence. As soon as you stop fabricating pressures for yourself you will stop exercising power over others. For if you act without pleasure, your actions reproach those around you and they won't be able to help building up resentment as they will feel to blame. This is the infernal circle often found in families.

One way and another, stress and the obligation it entails are the indirect equivalents of a direct takeover of power, and lead to the same resentment in those who are subjected to it.

***Question:*** *I feel out of harmony with my body. Diets and medicines don't help me. What should I do?*

***He says:*** Don't forget to look at yourself with a clear eye that leaves nothing out, that is to say a look that loves everything that is part of you.

There is something you haven't seen and it undermines you. It would be best if you found it yourself for you could accept the result of your own search but not one imposed on you from outside.

Look at your childhood tenderly, open yourself to it and go into it. If you accept it and give it your heart, it will entrust you with the key to a forgotten door. There you will find a secret knot that you have covered over with refusal and repressed tears.

Let go of the last strands that still bind you to desire for control, whether over events or the paths taken by those close to you. Let yourself be regenerated by the great and bountiful current of life without "willing" anything. If you can let yourself be swept off by it, you will find that you yourself are this current of life, free and joyous, that has all powers because it isn't separated from anything and heads towards complete fulfilment.

This letting-go, that can take place in relaxation and the calm of your depths, is one of the ways to give your body the chance to renew itself. It will stop you seeing yourself and others through a prism or grid of personal likes and dislikes that you want to impose on reality.

There is nothing special to do or to decide. You are the perfection of life. Don't prevent it from unfolding as it pleases. Then it will open all its secrets to you and you will be, for yourself and others, the movement itself both of everyday and universal creativity.

***Question:*** *Why is my life out of harmony with what I hope for? I am afraid of missing the opportunities my destiny offers.*

***He says:*** There is no way that you can miss the opportunities of your destiny. That maps itself out as your transformation progresses and reflects your actual state. If you don't meet anyone now it is because you are not yet ready to share your life with a companion. Even though you may not realize this, your subconscious records your states in depth. So you have nothing at all to worry about. Something beyond you guides you and takes you where you need to be, even if this sometimes seems difficult or unbearable.

Your choice of life was made long ago and allows you to evolve through vicissitudes that lead you towards yourself. In your work, a similar process is under way. You refuse what is offered because you cannot bear the reality of what it is. Pay great attention to yourself and observe very deeply your desire for something different: are you ready for a different job, for an apartment filled with light, for journeys and opportunities that lead towards freedom?

If what you dream of doesn't materialize, it is because fear is still a fetter. So the problem of fear must be dealt with first. Next, the problem of attachment. If inwardly you cut out the fear of not being able to pay your debts, you will be able to pay them because your inner freedom will stimulate opportunities for acceptable work, or an offer that you had not foreseen.

If in your most secret self you feel you are going to break out of your chrysalis, encourage this feeling, make it grow into reality.

When you have sorted out your problems of fear and attachments, visualize a place filled with light where you are happy to live. Visualize your well-being at all levels, whether it results from travel, work, or through meeting someone else, etc. But for this, your subconscious must be free of the past, free of fear and of all the layers of dross amassed for too long.

Trust your invisible strengths, they connect you to a different universe where everything is possible.

***Question:*** *Is shame linked to lying?*

***He says:*** Shame always results from an idea one has of how things "ought to be" in relation to oneself, to others or to a situation one submits to. If shame is felt through a lie one tells oneself or because the attitude of others is felt to be a lie, it becomes a suppressed injustice. Injustice or what seems to be injustice is a constant feature of life. But when the wound remains, and it has not been possible for the sensed injustice to be included in its implications, for it to be revealed or even immediately challenged, a slow deterioration can take place in the psyche. It is therefore absolutely essential to decypher its origins so that it leaves no after-effects.

Shame exists for a variety of reasons. It may result from a situation that is imposed on you and attacks your ego. In this case, expressing it as soon as possible frees you. Or it may spring from a word or an action that one regrets. There too, having the courage to express one's feelings clearly cleans up the situation because one can take account of the extent to which the ego is implicated in this kind of shame.

In your case, the ambiguity of other people's attitudes to you was experienced as cutting you off from your deep source, for you could neither express it nor clear things up. Your youth made that impossible. This state of affairs, often repeated, built up a climate of insincerity that separated you from your vital inner source. The ego, of course, was also involved, but at a stage in life when it needed to build itself up. The wound it then suffers causes it either to go astray or to inflate. A certain blindness sets in if you cannot relive and transcend this legacy of childhood.

The fact of recovering these events with absolute sincerity and total absence of judgement, and expressing them clearly together with their effect on you, will allow you to rediscover your lost source.

***Question:*** *What sort of new work could I undertake?*

***He says:*** You ask if you should go here or there, change your job, your life, or the way you think about your ambition. But your actions are only the reflection of your depths. So therefore it is at your depths that you could look clearly. What is the meaning of your existence? Why do these questions surface at this precise moment? Have you reached a crossroads, a new stage, new maturity? For a moment go into the silence of quiet attention and look at yourself with love, trust and clarity. Look for what is really important to you, in what field you would find yourself most surely.

In your heart is a longing to share, weariness with social success. You would like to spread the inner wealth that has been given you, and use your gift of communication to serve others as well as yourself. In other words you want to widen your horizons and be actively involved in the transformation which is under way on the earth.

You want your gifts to be useful, and not lie idle, for you know that in offering them you set free other people's abilities and goodwill.

You sense that something in yourself is lying idle. It is time to open up your hidden treasures, to be daring and trust your underlying strengths. By choosing a direction which truly suits you, an essential part of yourself will light up. At the same time you will see that different worlds can reveal themselves and you could surprise yourself by walking down the uncharted paths of new inspiration.

***Question:*** *I am crushed by material tasks and bones of contention from the past that leave me very heavy responsibilities. I feel left to face this problem alone for those who, to my way of thinking, should help me don't do so.*

***He says:*** The past weighs heavily on your shoulders. Don't let yourself be crushed by it, for its only reality is what you give it. Shake off the burden that so encumbers you, without any sense of guilt. You are not being asked to take on the chores of the whole family. You shut yourself into duty and so become resentful, for you know very well that others will take advantage of it. Let go of the vision you have of life as being heavy and full of constraints. You are free. Of course there are material tasks that need doing, but if you change the way you look at them, they can turn into a tool for your development and the measure of your inner success. Open the other door of your soul, the one you haven't seen, and you will discover unknown treasures. The greatest present one can give others and also oneself is to be happy. It is so simple to open oneself to the beauty of springtime, to the feeling of one's feet on the wet earth, to the unity of life.

Accept calmly what you cannot change in your life. It may be a lifeline thrown out by destiny to deepen your understanding of your secret being. It is in you that you will find joy and unimaginable wealth, but for this to happen, the ties of dependence on others will need to have been cut. What they say, think or do doesn't matter. Develop in yourself the jewel, inner freedom that allows you to live fully, and realize that what weighs heavy on you can become an opening for your transformation. If you can, change duty into love and expect nothing from anyone, or else entrust all your constraints to an image that is greater than you. If you are sensitive to the divine, it can take on your burdens and free you to live to your fullest without fear or guilt. It will lead you towards the unpredictable and joyful lands your soul hopes for. Then you will experience the upsurge and blessings of a new birth.

***Question:*** *My romantic relationships are always a bit shaky. What do I need to learn from this difficulty?*

***He says:*** Your emotional relationships are not yet entirely clear. You are attracted to partners who ask you to sort things out and that is where difficulties arise. You are looking for an ideal relationship in which you can remain wholly free. But in the world of duality this struggle is subtly aggravated where an intimate relationship is involved. There you are given the chance to bring to light very deep knots that have not yet been disentangled.

Very determined people seek, without realizing it, to flush out something vague in your way of seeing things and ask you, always subconsciously, to state where you think you are going. So they refer you back to yourself for you to express very clearly what you feel and what you want, without trying to escape from clear choices by silence or evasive speech. At the same time, your partners need to moderate their desire to influence you, since it irritates them to find ground which, in their eyes, is not firm. As they have the impression of not really being able to grasp you, they reinforce their will over you. So for them it becomes an opportunity to see what lies behind their instinctive desire for control or for domination and to distance themselves from it. If together you want to see yourselves clearly and to look at the interplay of problems the relationship highlights, it will be possible to build a different relationship where each accepts the other just as they are. But if some blindness remains on either side, it is better not to persist.

Generally speaking one notices the other's blindness more easily than one's own. One is imprisoned by one's own way of seeing from which it is very difficult to escape. But in fact, all ways of seeing are good as long as one accepts other people's.

In a relationship, adjustment between a couple is one of the most difficult lessons to face because in addition, there are the hazards of everyday life. The solution of conflict in this area is never found on the horizontal plane of duality. It can only emerge when we let go of our ego at least for long enough to view things from a different level of awareness.

***Question:*** *Should I envisage the possibility of a new relationship with a partner or have I already learnt all that I can from this kind of relationship?*

***He says:*** If you still think about a relationship of this sort it is because you have not entirely exhausted your desire to find unity in a couple. This natural desire can lead you into unforeseeable paths of divine love.

Live fully in your awaiting, don't reject it even if it

weighs on you a bit. Denying it won't make it disappear. See what it has to teach you, use it to understand and go forward on your own path. Don't let it take control, or divide you and hinder you from living. Enter fully into your desire, and not into searching for the object of this desire. When it has shown you yourself more clearly it will disappear. Then, either you will meet the partner who is right for you or else you will meet yourself in the clear core that no longer needs anyone because it is connected to everyone and everything.

***Question:*** *I need light to be shed on my future path in life. I am at a turning point and tormented by anxiety.*

***He says:*** You are wandering in a featureless country, a windowless house. Leave it, get out of the mental circuit that imprisons you. Blow away the vapours that fill your head.

You need to feel that your feet are in firm contact with the earth so that your roots can revive and nourish the whole of you. Then your activities will stop being so agitated and will be of more use to you.

Go into deep relaxation as often as possible so that you find your inner voice once again. That is what can guide you infallibly. Sink into the quiet that gives rise to all happiness.

This action can sometimes appear completely still and yet transform you from within.

You excel in the world of ideas and words, but they have no power because they swell up with a separate life and do not serve your essential being. They move around in an illusory world that is not connected to your true needs.

All work that links you with down-to-earth reality will benefit your development. See to it that your ideas lead to tangible results, to practical improvements in your life-style. In this way you will no longer be separated, no longer divided between mind, body and spirit. You will find once again the unpredictable ways of the heart, and for you the dance of life will be the dance of the universe.

Through gathering your instinctive strengths which are great, and integrating them into the divine current—the current of life— you will be able to change your very substance. Then your view of the world and of yourself will be transformed and you will be able to launch into the unknown of your new path in life. Today you cannot imagine the country it leads you towards. It is a country one cannot describe for it is always new, and so is the joy which bathes it in sunlight.

***Question:*** *How can I get rid of the constant control that prevents me living and letting my gifts blossom?*

***He says:*** The control you exert over yourself and that prevents you from breathing freely stems from a very deep fear. You haven't yet been able to look at yourself as you are because you judge yourself harshly. To understand your own workings fully it is vital to give up any form of judgement.

As a start, the solution for you is to love yourself just as you are, to look at the control and be at peace with it, accepting it completely as part of yourself. You take it into you with all the tenderness you are capable of, for in this love it will be able to surrender and show you the fear that lies hidden behind it.

Then go into the fear without refusing it. If you can come up to it quietly you will see it is not so terrible. Once you have touched the kernel of your fear, which is chiefly dependence on what others think of you, you will really come into yourself. You will understand the reason for your barricades. It is always love that is able to break them down and gather up the pieces of yourself; love of yourself as much as love of others (but this does not apply to projections of the ego). You will then learn to accept yourself and not make such demands either on yourself or on others.

By opening your hands to what you are, without using your will to escape it, a mutation will take place deep within you.

Let the part of you that does not seek power help you and let it invade you. This part is neither the brain, nor the intellect, nor the will. It is another light that carries you beyond the known. It burns up everything that clutters you. It connects you.

In silence and relaxation you can learn to listen. Then you will get to know your "inmost being" and your true richness. Your transformation begins there, because in the inmost being is no division whatever.

Every day you need a time for contemplation free from agitation or stress, so that you get to know the wonderful world within you. It contains the earth's most beautiful song and it will enable you to express it, not only with the voice, but also through the events and actions in your life.

***Question:*** *Who am I?*
*(This question is asked by someone who is torn between a highly developed rational side and extraordinary gifts as a healer.)*

***He says:*** This vital question for all human beings is particularly relevant for you as you utterly refuse to acknowledge the place of your origins where you were not separated from universal consciousness.

These two warring sides of yourself are nevertheless two branches of one tree.

The solution for you is to visualize your roots. Don't look further for the moment. Go down into the earth of your depths where you will find peace and serenity. What are you afraid of?

Only by going into your roots will you be able to achieve unity and set off again vertically for the stars. Only in this way can all the branches of your personality be reconciled.

You live in a horizontal world and find yourself in contact with illness, anxiety and the miasmas that humanity allows to ferment over the earth. Yours is the wonderful gift of being able to heal and relieve pain, but you forget the vertical element that allows you to hand over power to that which surpasses you.

In verticality is found the meaning of your life, because in its movement you can reconcile your rational tendencies with your gifts as a visionary messenger.

When you are able to say: I shall let love heal me and heal others through me, you will be completely protected, transformed and unified because in this state there is no longer either conflict or personal power.

Are you afraid of losing control? But what does that little bit of control amount to? If you can be part of the stream of life dancing everywhere over the earth and elsewhere, you no longer need power because you are the creative power. But when you create entities that frighten you, you are subjected to your own power which is the will for separation.

Let the liberating breath of love penetrate right into you and you will no longer be afraid, either of madness, or of death, or of suffering. Love is to be found through deep relaxation and detachment. It, non-separation, is the universal current.

If your gifts transcend you, it is because they are showing you the way of transcendence. Accept being much more than you are and at the same time being nothing more than the instrument of your own transcendence. To accept your own transcendence is to give up the limited power of your ego. It also means getting to a land of wonder that never ceases to transform you and lets you discover free and limitless space.

Consent to be reborn, for joy is calling you.

***Question:*** *What should I do in life?*

***He says:*** You would like practical and down-to-earth advice to hide your great yearning for a genuine pursuit of the absolute. Don't imagine that the practical world or your career can stand in the way of my coming. Whatever work or activities you undertake, all doors are open. There are no bars anywhere. It is simply that you shut yourself into illusory circles to subdue your fear.

One day you will open your eyes and wonder how such obvious joy could be concealed for so long.

You are always colliding with the difficulties you invent to protect yourself from anything that might sweep you towards that threatening world, the world of love. Its presence is troubling and you haven't got the key to expressing it, for love was cruelly lacking in your childhood. Now you would like to control it but you don't much understand its workings and are afraid of letting yourself be swallowed up.

If, witholding nothing, you allow yourself to be invaded, letting flow the innumerable streams of the compassion that is your true nature, you will know the unbounded bliss of those who are freed from fear because they have found me.

You ask me what you must "do" with your life. You already feel guilty about the choices you might consent to. Open your hands to what gives you pleasure. Accept life in the present moment, as it comes. Whatever decisions are taken, they will lead you infallibly to the place where you have decided to meet me. You know me well and have been aware of it for a long time.

Discover the window you have forgotten to open. It looks onto a marvellous garden that is you. In this garden it is so simple to love.

***Question:*** *Why is the Catholic Church, as a social institution, opposed to the present research into new levels of consciousness?*

***He says:*** The Catholic Church is an organization that is a support to people who need an established structure to lean on. It imposes dogmas and rules which must not be questioned. This confers on it power that it cannot renounce without renouncing its very existence. Research into new levels of consciousness allows people to distance themselves from these dogmas and rules, for they discover in themselves the personal path that leads to the light.

Once they decide not to lean on this established structure any longer, they find new liberty that releases them from all externally imposed systems. Then they can choose their own spiritual conditioning, but they know that it is but a conditioning and can be abandoned for a different one if necessary. They notice that today's truth can be seen as illusion tomorrow.

This absolutely does not suit the Church (as a structure based on fixed principles). It loses its power and has no other way to protect itself than brandishing anathemas and threats, as it actually dare not relax its inflexibility for fear it might disintegrate. It can only evolve extremely slowly and it is very hard for it to admit that it is not the only pathway to God.

Present day research is a frightening opening up that takes away from the Church all means of control. What is more, this research threatens to draw away many sincere seekers. But once the pilgrim has met himself in his core of light, the question of whether or not to belong to an organized Church does not arise. It has lost its importance. The pilgrim is then free either within the dogma and rules or in spite of them, just as he is free in any of life's circumstances because divine inspiration illumines and protects him.

***Question:*** *Why have I caused a car accident?*

***He says:*** The accident was caused by an inner tension that had no other way to express itself.

You have made a constant effort to hide your feelings about a situation you disapprove of, but that stays imbedded in you like a thorn in the foot. You keep on walking, but a moment comes when you can no longer bear it, especially when a new event reactivates and exacerbates the problem.

As you have no way of dealing with the difficulty directly or even of speaking openly to those who are concerned, protest settles in at the level of the unconscious. You haven't been able to let off steam in the normal course of events and the accident is like an explosion that releases it in a single stroke.

See to it that you express yourself as freely as is possible, and never let resentment or disapproval build up. This will release you, and it can also release others, for they don't always understand why there is a cloud overshadowing the relationship.

To speak about what disturbs you, what you find hard to bear, is a safeguard. You can always express it with delicacy and tact, choosing the right moment. Never let even the least thing left unsaid fester in you. Be open about your feelings: your fear, your rebellion, your desires. In such a state of truth and transparency you will not only avoid accidents, but also uneasiness in everyday life. This will bring you closer both to inner unity and to the "essence" of being that is the true expression of yourself.

***Question:*** *The future frightens me, how can I find reassurance?*

***He says:*** Don't be worried. I am the infinite Source of Love in you. Spread it around you from moment to moment and it will come back to you. If you must think about the future see it as light flooding from everywhere.

Open your hands to what is given and all that happens to you will be good. You will see that events reflect what is in you and that they help you journey towards your essential being.

Nothing can resist love and if you release this inner source and let it gush out, you will be wholly protected.

In love no harm can reach you because you are not "separated". You possess the whole universe, so are no longer tied to particular possessions, whether they are material, emotional, intellectual or spiritual. This doesn't mean that you have to reject these "possessions", on the contrary: live fully, a day at a time, accepting all that life brings you, but don't hold on to anything. Stay open to joy, whatever the circumstances. Listen quietly to your inner voice, it will be your surest guide. To hear it, look clearly into yourself without judging, but also without overlooking a single corner of the cupboard where your ghosts are hidden. Then you will discover new strengths and a keen awareness of what to do.

I never leave you and am wholly present for you alone because I am the unity in your heart and my Love for you is total.

***Question:*** *What does psychoanalysis signify and is it useful?*

***He says:*** Psychoanalysis has its uses but it does not sort out all difficulties. It is a point of departure, an initiation to getting to know oneself, but there is often a temptation to get stuck in it. It has enabled certain taboos to be discredited. For many human beings the ferment of these taboos caused madness or self-destruction. At its best, it includes listening and a detached, non-judgemental approach, in which those who suffer can find the space they need to come to a new understanding of themselves.

The coming times will see another form of therapy develop. It will not be based solely on the analysis of behaviour. Instead problems will be placed in a much wider context. It will not concentrate on one aspect of personality rather than another. It will be part of a greatly expanded reality and will guide the patient towards integrating into "human nature" in its totality or even into nature at a universal level. This new form of therapy will lead the human being to readjust to the general current of life. It will help not only those who are ill, but also every so-called normal person to find authenticity and their place in this world.

Whenever one person discovers his or her destination and happiness, others are helped to do the same. It is like a puzzle where each piece that finds its place facilitates the forming of the whole picture.

***Question:*** *Is ambition necessary in order to fulfil one's life. If not how does one make use of this energy?*

***He says:*** Ambition, for many people, is a driving force enabling them to fulfil themselves completely on the level of duality. Ambition to succeed, to express oneself, to make money, etc., drives most of us to exert ourselves and when one is young, it is rare not to be quite swept along by it. Ambition should not be judged in any way. But if a person's deep inner being has set out for a goal other than power, money or success, ambition has no justification. It would then act as a brake, because all the desires of the ego become impediments on the path of evolution, especially if they are not seen clearly. Even those who claim to be on a spiritual path do not always notice that this path itself is sometimes obscurely coveted as a possession or a source of power. One has only to observe the degree to which rivalries are exacerbated among the followers of certain "masters". This allows each of them to become aware of their own avidity.

At the horizontal level of duality, there are ways of using this energy differently by putting it to the service of all. For instance: my ambition is to make money not only to please myself, as well as those around me, but also to aim more widely and distribute my money for the benefit of humanity in general. Money, viewed in this way, no longer produces feelings of disgust (money is dirty), of secrecy (I am ashamed of having it) or of guilt. It becomes a way of transmitting love.

A similar process can be imagined with the ambition for success or for power: why not enjoy one's success and at the same time serve the planet?

Vigilance, where ambition is concerned, is always needed because it is not separated from the ego and desire for power. In journeying towards the light, we progressively hand over power to what transcends us. In order to find the "beyond" in ourselves, the openness that leads to "divine space", there is no need for that sort of baggage. Ambition can then dissolve at the same time as fear and guilt in the quiet accomplishment of a life that is fulfilled.

It seems we can't avoid the pitfalls and lessons life gives us through what we are. Letting-go one's grip becomes much easier with age, especially when the different stages of life have been accepted, understood and recast in the crucible of the intelligence and the heart.

***Question:*** *What is the relevance of moral rules and are there times when one can dispense with them?*

***He says:*** Morality is very useful in everyday life and indeed for most of us as long as the "inner guide" has not been found. This means that we are not yet in contact with the hidden reality that is our own true self. Rules that belong to the social order and derive from those of the religious order still give cohesion to our structures, at least in appearance. In fact, however, most often in life only lip-service is paid to them.

Lying, therefore, is the real problem, for lies conceal themselves behind the rules and undermine the very foundations of morality that would otherwise be legitimate. Morality is used very often as nothing more than a shield to cover over hypocrisy.

When you operate by means of pretence (saying or thinking one thing, but doing another, etc.), division increases and you stray away from Love which is Unity.

Have the courage to be what you are and to start your journey from your basic reality. If you don't, the discrepancy grows ever wider and you cannot understand why the bars of your cage close in on you.

Nothing can be transformed if you have not seen, understood and accepted what is in you. When you deny this basic evidence, a moral code plastered over your failure to see clearly is nothing but a parody and prevents spiritual opening. Many of us live like this as it makes for socially acceptable behaviour. You then rely on rules that reassure you but do not solve your initial problem.

When integrity is applied to all levels of being, when it reaches even the most hidden recesses, you no longer need a moral code imposed from outside because your own ethic takes over. Then openness becomes possible. It lets you make contact with your essence, the divine spark that connects you to yourself, to others and to the universe. You discover a new earth where Love takes root and can flower in the sunshine of true freedom, for you have changed your level of awareness.

***Question:*** *I do too many things and become separated from myself. How can I stop myself going faster and faster?*

***He says:*** It is not what you "do" that is important at the moment, for your activities derive from increasing stress that cuts you off from yourself. Stop whenever possible, find your rhythm again and your serenity.

When you lose yourself in too many activities, nothing gives pleasure any longer. Offer yourself the gift of happiness in the most insignificant events of daily life and you will see your problems melt quietly in the sunshine of your joy. Make each movement slower, but let it fulfil itself and extend into the world of light that is another aspect of our world.

Whenever you are stressed or irritated you lose your soul and the opportunity to "link" with the divine smile that transforms your destiny. Don't project judgement on either yourself or your actions for judgement only divides you and prevents Love. Nothing more is asked of you than to live and be happy because your happiness is a gift for you and also for those around you. It spreads without your even being aware of it. It is simple and wonderful to be alive if you don't construct mountains for yourself out of rules and obstacles.

You are not obliged to undertake so many things or to entertain so many people. Forget all the agitation that separates you from your source; pace yourself by gentleness and well-being. They are your best guides.

***Question:*** *How can one make choices in all areas of life?*

***He says:*** We are faced with making choices at every moment of life and we are often quite unaware of doing so. But when we have to make important decisions, instinct is sometimes weakened and the mind takes over.

We weigh up the pros and cons, go from one solution to another while calculating the positives and the negatives. This commonly used method is not always the best when issues involve a vital commitment, for the choice then takes place at a superficial level.

A person's deep-seated motivations are not located in the realm of the mind or reason. Reason can be used as a support, but important choices are made with different faculties when they are in harmony with a "true" orientation. What someone feels to be their truth at a given moment then corresponds exactly with the choice that has been made.

What are these faculties that can help us choose? They come to light in a relaxed body and mind, when the parasites of a hectic life have been shed. In such a state of quietness, it is possible to find in oneself a different current that puts one in contact with a sort of "inner silence" which is the best of counsellors.

You wonder whether to change your job, start or break up a relationship, emigrate, and so on. Without brooding over the question, let it live with you for several days, free from the sort of anxiety that stops you letting it breath in you.

By allowing the question to mature peacefully, the answer will come to you. It will appear suddenly and seem obvious because you will have entrusted the problem to that "beyond" of yourself that is not your ego. It is as if you changed your usual mechanism of nervous tension to call on different strengths. These strengths will never let you down for they are the essence of yourself and know what suits you.

***Question:*** *Why does the state of being a victim so often turn into the state of being a tormentor? Why does the victim-turned-tormentor pick on a fresh victim instead of confronting the original tormentor? How can one break the links of this terrible chain?*

**He says:** The state of being a victim very often turns into that of being a tormentor because the two states are interdependent. If there is no victim there is no tormentor and *vice versa*.

In every tormentor there is a past or future victim. Both these roles result from the same aberration. When a person consents to be a victim he unconsciously and implicitly consents to be a tormentor. The only way to stop this infernal chain is first to become aware of it.

In the concentration camps Nazi tormentors carried the horror to the lengths of giving institutional status to a tendency that is more or less latent in each one of us, and this they did in the name of an ideology. Here, the perversion is doubled, for the ideology invests it with a sort of respectability that gets transmitted to the unconscious. This then clothes sadistic actions with improper legitimacy.

Victims who become tormentors rarely choose their tormentor as a victim, except when vengeance has been carefully nurtured. Usually, it is because the victim has no other resource than to revenge himself on someone weaker or someone likely to submit to his power. The case of the policeman who abuses his power because he is having marital difficulties is well known.

To break the fateful chain of victim-tormentor-victim it is absolutely essential to understand clearly that the process is also at work in oneself and decide once and for all to stop it. A clear look at what we ourselves are, even if it is unpleasant to face, will make it possible to end this infernal cycle. For at a more general level and in everyday situations that seem relatively insignificant, we play our part in these same power relationships. We are not always conscious of our little daily sadisms. Through impartial and honest observation we can sort out this problem in ourselves, and break with the perversion utterly. Rigour and honesty with oneself are, as always, our surest means of discovering our own mechanisms and of being prepared to change the ways we operate.

Contrary to what many people imagine, it is possible to extricate oneself from power relationships. But the door lies in us, and it opens onto another level of awareness. At this level, power relationships disappear because the ego is reduced to its simplest form. It no longer needs to inflate itself with its importance because the self is growing. The self never needs to show off, for it really is the essence of life and of what we are. The self or, if we prefer it, the divine in ourselves, is the element of light that can resolve all problems and we can trust it whatever our difficulties are. But for the self truly to grow, the basic essential is to get to know the workings of our  ego. This needs total sincerity and absence of all judgement. It is a exercise for each instant that can fill a whole life.

***Question:*** *What does forgiveness mean and what effect can forgiveness have on our physical and moral health?*

***He says:*** To forgive means to get rid of resentment and of everything that prevents love from circulating freely.

Forgiveness is a present one gives oneself. A gift of healing on the moral plane that results, very often, in healing on the physical plane. By forgiving yourself to begin with, you eliminate guilt, a major obstacle to the birth of joy.

After that, it becomes easier to forgive others.

When forgiveness is sincere and total, it leads gently to another way of understanding. You realize that when there is no judgement, there is no longer any reason for forgiveness. When you can give up all judgement, you draw nearer to unity. This allows one of the principal causes of suffering to disappear.

You then shatter the framework of rigid thinking that often comes from a moral straightjacket and not from your deep source which is Love.

When you carry out this work on yourself, you free the earth from a weight of hatred and negativity. How can you complain about others who massacre each other and make war when you yourself are not free from thoughts of violence, power, resentment or possessiveness?

You are not really aware of the fact that collective thought has an immediate impact on the material reality of what takes place on earth.

The negative bludgeoning loosed on us daily by newspapers, television and radio amounts to an insidious disintegration disastrous for our psychic powers. It latches on to everything divisive. It works on our greed and frustration and we are shown up at our sorriest and most depressing. This is true of most of it though there are a few attempts to represent us more positively.

We have to change this reflection of what we are at the moment by initiating a transformation in our way of thinking, of living and of loving. By allowing ourselves to be swallowed up by the image the media sends back to us, we irremediably put an end to all hope of harmony and happiness on earth. Each one of us is responsible for the events that disfigure our world. Forgiveness is the start of a way that lights up. Along it lies the possibility of unforeseeable happiness, the secret of new equilibrium.

It is comforting to realize that each one of us has the means of transforming ourselves and so can contribute to the protection and healing of the sick earth.

## Chapter Two

# Sexuality

***Question:*** *What stands in the way of my expressing myself freely?*

***He says:*** You have realized that through getting to know your sexuality and letting it flower, you could undertake a different journey, one where life bursts out in you. By ridding your depths of the narrow morality you have breathed since childhood and plunging happily into the source of what you are, which is the divine impulse, you will blend into the song of life and express its fullness and subtlety.

Let this force rise. It cries out at being strangled or turned aside instead of being accepted in its beauty, as if the very word sexuality sprouted the devil's horns. The prohibitions and rules born of fear, and the straightjacket imposed by religions, prevent you from opening yourself to love.

Unless sexuality is accepted love becomes warped, for it cannot get through to its roots. Even divine love cannot exist without sexuality. It would then be nothing but illusion or mirage. The notion of impurity usually associated with the word is an aberration that breeds secrecy, fantasies and guilt. Moreover, any notion of impurity sets the mechanism going.

Through discovering the beauty and purity of this force that can fill you completely, you will be able to sing without constraint, in harmony with yourself and with the joy of life's origins.

***Question:*** *How can I feel more in harmony with myself?*

***He says:*** You have lost the connection with love. But you can find it again through sexuality if you lose yourself in it, letting go of control and going down to the roots of primordial exultation. It can be the crucible of your transformation as long as there is no desire either for power or seduction. Your body is full of tears, tears that the child choked back. Plunge into those tears so that you recognize them and love them. Love whatever happens to you, love your past, your present and your future without fear of suffering or of being misunderstood. Let go of the structures that prevent you finding the heart of what you truly are: an outpouring of love when it is no longer divided but expresses life itself.

Your life blood is held back by a sort of construct, a mental shield to protect you from the outside world. But this protection itself is what prevents you opening up to new joy. Acceptance of being just what you are, of being no more than those tears you didn't want, will break through the shell that cuts you off from others and from yourself.

In acceptance you will find the transparency and fluidity that allow you to act in the ever fresh current of your creativity. Your creativity is very great and springs from sexuality. But it will not be able to express itself consistently and fully unless you live your sexuality differently. If the transmutation comes from your roots, you will again be in contact with the original forces of divine love, or of human love which, when you are aware of unity, comes to the same thing.

***Question:*** *Is it possible for an experience of the absolute to be revealed through the relationship of a couple? And is there a connection between this experience and sexuality?*

***He says:*** Experience of the absolute is omnipresent because we ourselves are the absolute and any state or event in our lives can put us into "living" contact with this fact. But certain essential aspirations of our existence allow us to experience the Unity more easily.

You could say that the marriage of heaven and earth becomes possible when the created being rediscovers its universal dimension, its fusion with the divine. Curiously enough, religions with their prohibitions often get in the way of one finding God because of the guilt they virtually instil where instincts and the body are concerned. When the rising of vital impulses is sullied by thoughts of sin, is diverted into secrecy and separated from impulses of the soul, division between body and spirit becomes inevitable. How then can one live the experience of the whole? We are riddled with this education:

for so many centuries it has weighed on us, and it is very difficult to eliminate notions of sin and the forbidden that have been nurtured since childhood. When we judge, conceal or repress the sexual impulse we repudiate an important part of ourselves. We deprive ourselves of a means of evolving, for this energy if it is accepted, lived and transcended, can lead to new capacities of transformation. It can also open up the way to a different vision, bliss in our lives that up till now we have ignored.

People, with their narrow-mindedness and senseless fear, have diverted the life blood of their instinctive nature and channelled it into secrecy, taboo and misery.

Everything in human nature can be simple and sacred. But rigid thinking pollutes, deforms and corrupts the natural movement of life. It shuts life up in rules and wants to control whatever goes beyond it.

The inevitable reaction to this nowadays is that moral standards are relaxed. This relaxation also cuts us off from our roots and deflects sexuality from its capacity to reach another level of reality.

The sexual impulse, primordial power, can lead us to ourselves and, when it flowers freely and in clear light, this means to the divine.

In a human couple the "marriage of heaven and earth" is very rare because the human couple is caught up in mutual attachment. Attachment based on the ego's expectations fetters Love. The relationship of "power-submission" or "security-fear-duty" stifles the freedom needed to discover common space. But when partners are not set on the idea that the other ought to be different, when they can evolve side by side without constraint, they can discover in both themselves and the other new identity and autonomy. It is only when two beings can accept each other just as they are, that the marriage of heaven and earth becomes possible. The union then opens onto the infinite and the divine dimension is not different from human love.

***Question:*** *I feel a victim of fate and do not know how to resolve my problems, especially those related to a sexuality I cannot accept. What should I do?*

***He says:*** Do you believe fate exists? If you do, then it does. If you don't, then you already have everything you need to sort out your problems.

Take courage and look into the cellar where you locked away the tears, the frustration, the taboos of your childhood. Have the courage to be "one" with your impulses, whatever they are. This is the only way to defuse hatred, jealousy or other emotions that are difficult to bear.

You have buried everything that you reject because of the judgement you inflict on yourself. But by what law do you decide: this is good, that is bad? Something in you has allowed itself to get shut into the rules of a moral code that advocates hypocrisy and the refusal of what actually exists. Look clearly, without judging, at what goes on in you. Be reconciled with the whole of yourself. Only by acknowledging your truth can you initiate your transformation.

Sexuality is part of the truth that you reject. You have set up an ideal and won't accept what diverges from it. But as you couldn't accept the ground as it was before being worked on, the transformation can't take place and the body reflects what you repress in your unconscious. It is as if you insisted on digging in the air a foot or so above the earth. Be at one with your sexuality as it is, without any guilt.

You will see that it is the power of love, the desire for union, the desire to complete each other, to lose oneself in unity with the other. This power doesn't let itself be tamed, especially if you deny it. It is beautiful and pure and can lead us to ourselves and to the divine.

In breaking out of your taboos, at least in your mental images, you will find liberty and that wild joy, the eternal dance of life. This vital force that rises in you must be acknowledged and loved before you can transcend it. Lies are a minefield on which you can build nothing.

***Question:*** *Why am I cut off from my sexuality?*

***He says:*** Narrow-minded secular or religious education that instils guilt has paralyzed most of those over a certain age. Prohibitions and taboos concerning the body were encouraged and built up by the religions and so permeated the atmosphere and everyday life that they have totally scrambled our instincts and turned sexuality into the sin of sins.

By allowing everything that touches even remotely on sex to fester away in silence, in shame and in secret, we reject our opportunities for happiness in an important area of life. Nowadays the opposite reaction leaves us just as unhappy and frustrated because the capacity to unite love and sex has so often been lost sight of.

A fundamental error was made when, in the name of the divinity, we renounced that part of ourselves. It is as though we had sullied and refused what God gave us, when sexuality lived in love is one of the direct ways of merging with the divine, for it participates in the process of creation.

It is never too late to change one's view of oneself and the world. Dare to open yourself completely to surrender and love, it is the only way to return to your sexuality.

You might discover that whatever you live in joy and freedom brings you nearer to God, for then you are in perfect harmony with yourself, and that means connected to the whole.

***Question:*** *What can be done when sexual impotence sets in and makes one aggressive?*

***He says:*** Sexual impotence often results from some form of guilt. In the West, sexuality entails basic guilt, and this is reinforced in families where religion is repressive. But at the same time sexuality in a man is considered a measure of strength at every level. So when these two tendencies clash, especially as a man grows older, impotence is almost inevitable.

His companion will need a lot of patience and tact to help him to wipe out the result of this conflict as far as possible. If she can appreciate his worth in all walks of life, let him know how useful he is, and discover with him areas where he is indispensable, he might well recover his virility.

At the same time if she can lovingly take his hand to lead him away from guilt and show him the straightforward path of life that forgives us our mistakes, she will ease his anxiety or aggression. Sexuality is not separated from life. At all levels of being it is involved far more deeply than one imagines, but despite apparent liberation there are still many taboos. Forgiveness is the key to all healing, though forgiving oneself is often the most difficult. Through forgiveness of the mistakes one has inevitably made at some time or other, energy can once again flow freely as much in one's body as in one's psyche and mind.

Sexuality freely accepted without preconceived ideas, that is released from moral or religious prisons and able to express itself without fear or taboos, can carry within it the sense of creation and transcendence. Then it can be lived harmoniously for it results from the balance of physical, emotional and spiritual forces.

***Question:*** *How can one live one's sexuality successfully? (Question asked by a woman.)*

***He says:*** Love and trust are the keys to flowering in this area just as they are in almost all areas of life. First of all to trust oneself and to love oneself just as much as one trusts and loves the other. We suffer in the West from repression that has been practised for many hundreds of years. Even birth instils basic guilt that the unconscious finds it very difficult to get rid of. The Churches reinforce this guilt, especially those advocating celibacy for priests, as if the devil hid himself in all sexual desire. Very often the abstinence required of them results in transgression or in mental overactivity that lends exaggerated importance to the act. So, through the influence of these priests, something that is simple and natural becomes tinged with the sulphurous colour of "sin" and induces many of us to deflect or restrict our opportunities for legitimate and healthy pleasures. The exaggerated emphasis placed on the act thus separates it from life.

***Question:*** *How can the beauty of this longing for bodily union be experienced?*

***He says:-*** Simply by letting oneself drown, by abandoning oneself utterly to the union of souls. This union has no diabolical connotations, and when it is total it is easier to let the body go along with it. Duality, separation are always what prevent us from living. The body's fervour can express the soul or conversely the soul's fervour can find its outlet through the body.

Education has led us so far off course that we are no longer in contact with our body and often deny it. It then takes its revenge either by becoming blocked or by falling ill. If one is not at ease with one's own body, it is very difficult to feel at ease with anyone else's. So first one has to work on oneself: to change one's attitude to the act that gives life; to delight in being a woman; to be happy to be loved and desired; to accept the pleasure of one's body as a gift from heaven, a gift of creation, and to let it flower without fear or control.

It is also through abandoning control that physical pleasure can spread its wings. If it is stripped of any guilt, it will become the divine expression of our nature, and so the expression of love.

***Question:*** *Is it possible to discover the divine dimension if one is cut off from one's sexuality?*

***He says:*** Don't think that sexuality is indispensable to encountering God. God can be sensed in any of life's experiences or simply in the air you breathe, in a child's eyes, the scent of a rose or the song of rain on the roof of your house. Don't attach God to one thing rather than another, but also don't exclude him from anything at all. Grace is fluid, touching all the faces of life with light. It is our mind that deforms us and makes what we are ugly.

To find the divine, sexuality is not specially at issue, but the lie you are often tempted to tell yourself in this sphere leads you to the illusion that is always a dead-end on the path of your evolution. You only need to look clearly and courageously at what is going on inside you. Are you trying to sublimate your frustration through fear of living or of being inadequate? Or, on the contrary, do you blame yourself in relation to your partner because you no longer find him attractive? Have you perhaps been persuaded through books or some other form of conditioning that one "must" or "must not" live one's sexuality?

Each time you get closer to your own truth, a surge of "awareness" allows you to climb a step towards the divine sun of your heart.

For a long time, sexuality has been the principal reservoir of our taboos. Now it has become sadly glutted with its own excess, devoid of either reason or love. These two opposites meet on the common ground of lies and insincerity as regards our essential reality. Whatever the aspects of your life may be, look at them and understand them with all your love.

With or without sexuality, the doors of the invisible elude what you long and hope for, but they'll open suddenly when you let yourself go.

And sometimes the most unexpected circumstances, even those that seem disastrous, lead you mysteriously into the divine arms.

Chapter Three

# The Psychic World

***Question:*** *Are my dreams important? Could they sometimes refer to previous lives or convey a spiritual message?*

***He says:*** Dreams have the importance and meaning that you give them. Some enlighten you about yourself, others can be prophetic and tell you about future events or the opening of new doors. But only you can really give them a meaning for they depend on a symbolic code whose key only you possess. Of course some dreams can be interpreted in a generalized way but the interpretations are never certain and above all they reflect the psychological criteria and evolution of the interpreter.

As in all professions that deal with the psyche, to gain power over the other person is both a temptation and a danger. So it is wiser to speak of your dreams as little as possible to anyone else. When you feel that they are important, live with them, carry them in the intimacy of your heart before searching them for their secret. In this osmosis the message that is transmitted can be understood at a much deeper level and you will not see things as intruding on your inner life. Another person obviously has different criteria from yours and would really need to be a "neutral" extension of yourself for you to listen to them with complete confidence.

If you foster mental images such as those of previous lives, you will have dreams that refer to previous lives—at least this is a possibility. If spiritual aspiration is your driving force, you will have messages to help you understand and develop this aspiration. By changing your outlook on your life and your dreaming, you could place them on the same level of reality or unreality and, for example, think of sleeping and waking as two faces of the same "illusion".

Give space to all the hypotheses and choose those that suit you. Whichever ones you choose, your dreams will support them. Sometimes they could indicate the orientation of the choices even before these are consciously adopted.

But never forget to let yourself be filled by the unfathomable light of the divine, where such questions melt into the unity of another level of consciousness.

***Question:*** *I am "clairvoyant" and wonder what is going on when cosmic entities seem to address others through me.*

***He says:*** These entities correspond to your inner reality and derive from your unconscious request. If your most intimate inner reality is absolute Love, this Love could manifest itself through an image that corresponds to you. In this way you would be able to speak in the name of a master or of cosmic entities. It is also possible that no image would be needed.

But if your inner reality is veiled by power, hatred or possessiveness, the entity that your unconscious projects will ask you or will ask others for actions that could be harmful or mad. To enable you to keep your power over others, some things that are true or flattering will be said and will destabilize those who listen to you all the more. You will have the impression of being guided from the beyond and weak souls will be in danger of venturing into a world where the mind deteriorates. You also expose yourself to considerable risks.

Many people allow themselves to be deluded by "mediums" or "clairvoyants" who have not carried out in themselves the work of self-knowledge that would eliminate deviations.

If this work has not been carried out, you expose yourself all in good faith to intermediary worlds that have nothing to do with the divine unity, even though the message that comes through may seem sound.

When, without knowing it, you are in the selfish power of the ego and you manipulate psychic powers, you connect yourself to a harmful astral world. You are then dangerous both to yourself and to others because you are dealing with powers that are greater than you and that you have no means of controlling.

Only love can guide you to the appropriate action and to understanding others. An immediate feeling of liberation, of well-being and of joy then spreads quite naturally all round you.

***Question:*** *How can one recognize the authenticity of some so-called "spiritual" experiences? How can one assess the quality of certain "masters", "mediums" or of groups for meditation and other practices that aim at the evolution of one's being.*

***He says:*** The answer to this question is very important. The present times are particularly unsettled and countless movements are coming into existence all around, some with genuine intentions, others whose aim is power or material interest.

When you take part in this type of gathering or seminar, observe the leader very carefully. Look at the way he behaves, his attitude to himself, to the others and to the "inner voice" that guides him. If you feel the person lives in accordance with his teachings and asks for little or no money, if you see him radiant, happy, with body, mind and spirit in harmony, then it is probable that you are in presence of someone you can trust.

When a "master", a medium, or the intermediary of a so-called personage in the beyond arrives with a swollen ego, and a following whose submission and flattery he encourages, watch out. Authenticity is in proportion to the integrity of the person. If someone is divided, meaning that he has neither accepted his body and his life, nor developed in himself the capacity to work out his own problems, how can you expect him to speak in the name of an evolved entity? The entity that inhabits him is no stranger to his subconscious. It reflects at depth his aspirations, his being, his secret reality. Sometimes the subconscious is in contact with an intermediary zone where our fears, our violence, our hatred and our taste for power materialize. It is therefore possible to meet sincere people who believe they have been entrusted with a "mission" when in fact they are the playthings of their subconscious. They run the risk of madness while causing a great deal of confusion around them.

But if you observe your own feelings carefully and at the same time observe the person who claims to be "inhabited" or who presents himself as a master, you will immediately know what is going on.

When you feel happy, in more intimate contact with yourself and the universe, and when your heart opens to a wider love, you can be sure that your encounter or the step you have taken is right and suits you perfectly.

***Question:*** *I feel guilty and have a menacing vision of Jesus. I feel doomed to go to Hell and suffer dreadfully. What can I do?*

***He says:*** If in your head you build up a figure of Jesus who is not filled with love, with compassion and with forgiveness, it is not Jesus. How can you imagine me as hard and cruel? How can you imagine God or Mary demanding your death? It is nonsense. Don't you realize that these demons you have constructed are projections of your suffering and uncertainty? All these negative entities calling for your death are the materialization of your fears and the shadows you carry within you. Come back to a life where you are peacefully concerned with yourself. Look for simplicity. Cast off this cruel and destructive imagery. You have understood that our beliefs make us what we are. So put away from you any beliefs that do not generate light and love.

Rebuild yourself gently as a precious edifice whose foundations are specially cared for. Then place on them a small stone and, without hurrying, another. Stop for a moment and envisage that it is possible to be happy, that it is possible to open yourself to the beauty of the earth, the beauty of life.

YOU ARE FORGIVEN

I, Jesus, say this to you.

The Christ of whom you speak is not real. I shall protect you from the future Hell that you think you have deserved. But above all help me to protect you from what you are living NOW.

I am close to you, a vessel of light and calm. Never forget to remedy things each time you feel threatened by negative entities, by realizing that they are nothing but a materialization of your guilt.

Hell is what you are living now. It has no reality outside yourself. Channels were opened in you before you were ready and your transformation has veered off into unbearable suffering. There has been a fissure between, on the one hand precise beliefs confined within a framework, and on the other, the immeasurable freedom that pushes on into the unknown. These two orientations cannot exist in you at the same time. To find peace you must let one of them go.

Either you turn to an organized religion that will support you and whose rules and tradition you accept, or, with no framework, you let yourself be swept up in the whirlwind of the unknown and let go of all your landmarks. Clearly, mixing the two results in appalling anxiety. If you let go of traditional landmarks, there is neither Hell nor Paradise nor Purgatory, and the deity takes the form that suits you. You live the unity in your own way and no longer cling to anything known. Then you will become aware of your freedom and never again will a phantasm be able to trouble you, because you will truly be yourself.

While waiting to be able to choose between these two orientations, live a congenial life close to the earth as simply as you can.

The earth is our mother and the more deeply rooted is our relationship with it, the freer is our soul to fly to the stars.

***Question:*** *Am I in danger? I feel threatened by both the physical and the astral world.*

***He says:*** This message will be of no use to you unless you are prepared to question yourself thoroughly, leaving no stone unturned, for the only danger that threatens you is your inner confusion.

Look at yourself clearly and let everything that is not transparent disappear. You are cluttered up with confused ideas that materialize outside of you. Wake up to the fact that it is your own fear that causes the danger.

We are our beliefs; so put some order into your beliefs. Forge them strongly with gold and light, and connect yourself directly to the highest, that means to the deepest part of yourself.

Avoid everything in your life that is not clear. Secrecy is not good for you. Avoid any relationships based on power, whether material, mental or even spiritual. Many people make use of a professed spirituality to exercise power. Keep clear of that kind of contact because you are vulnerable. Never try to find out about parallel worlds or psychic experiences. This is inappropriate for you, as you get drawn into unhealthy dependency. Straightforwardness and simplicity are your best guides. Have faith in a world without complications in which you can find stability. Root yourself as best you can in practical and useful activities. Through this the divine will be given to you because you will have rejected the incoherences that drew you away from your true nature. Rediscover in yourself Love's dazzling bough that neither asks nor expects anything of anyone. That bough will protect you from all dangers and will give you limitless joy.

***Question:*** *Why am I completely drained of vital energy when I am with certain people?*

***He says:*** If at some level of your being you are fragile, you give certain people the chance to invade you at that level. It is just as well to be aware of this because you could suffer serious harm on the psychic plane.

To protect yourself, all that is needed is to become active in the relationship, to be a transmitter instead of a receiver. If you are used to visualization, you can send a very bright current of blue light through the solar plexus. This helps the person to stay centred on themselves. They are unaware of what is happening. You do them a favour because when they infiltrate you they are out of harmony with their deep nature. All this happens at a level that is not accessible to them.

You could also imagine your own aura as a luminous egg without any crack. This will protect and strengthen you not only in your personal relationships, but also each time you go into relaxation or meditation. When your aura is entirely luminous, when it has no grey or spongy areas, you are not in danger of being infiltrated, and what is more, no serious illness can reach you.

When you have carried out these visualizations, connect yourself both very deep and very high as if you were a flame of joy rising from the centre of the earth to lose itself among the stars.

***Question:*** *What does mental illness signify, and what can I do to alleviate it?*

***He says:*** Madness often has its origin at the moment of a branching-off in a person's life. At some crucial period the future sufferer from mental illness has refused to look clearly at a situation or an inner state. His whole potential is then unconsciously used to find a dead end, a lie that will destroy him. It is as if his personality has turned against him and forced him to retreat into a cul-de-sac.

Fear is so great that he cannot accept help. That would once again face him with the obstacle he does not want to see.

The only thing you could do is to accept him as he is and to love him where he is, that is to say with his illness, his refusals, in his imprisonment. If you are very close to the sufferer, it may be possible to show him, not by words, but through love and understanding, that the original obstacle doesn't exist, that it is only an illusion. In going together over the course of his life, you may be able to find with him, if he has the trust, the moment he refused his own truth. What is important is not the desire to change him but rather to accompany him without expecting anything, either improvement or gratitude.

It is by simply placing your footsteps in his that you will be able to sense with him the reason for his refusal to live.

Compassion of this order is a gift which can transform the sick person and transform you yourself. It can also have an effect at the level of the whole, for we are not separate.

***Question:*** *What is the meaning of these circles and other mysterious figures that appear in fields at harvest time, a phenomenon that has been observed all over the planet for several years?*

***He says:*** These phenomena, inscribed over wide areas, are the symbol of the transformation of the earth in its relationship with the cosmos.

They are important signs and their meaning will be revealed at the moment when man's evolution allows it. In the meantime they prepare minds to accept that the earth is in conscious relationship with the rest of the universe.

The planet, in its marvellous trajectory, is linked to the infinite in a way that we can only conceive of by analogy. The earth is to the universe what a cell is to the human body. When the human body is transformed through the advent of new consciousness, the cell is affected. Similarly, when transformations take place at a cosmic level, signs can be perceived on earth. But such transformations set up chain reactions. These go in all directions and range from the infinitesimal to the infinitely great and vice-versa.

The human imagination is fascinated by this sort of phenomenon and wants either to turn it into a fairy tale, or button it up in rational explanations, or else to deny its existence by claiming that it is a hoax. But none of these differing attitudes is adequate and they merely show up the mind set of the observer who is incapable of observing even the slightest phenomenon without investing it with his own substance. He doesn't realize that he is part of the phenomenon and that his way of seeing is no more valid than other people's.

Without an observer, there are no observed phenomena. Therefore we are co-creators of all that our senses reveal to us and our objectivity is nothing but illusion.

## Chapter Four

# Suffering

*(To a young man who has Aids.)*

***He says:*** I am close to you, in you, I am wherever you need me and I can be born every instant. Don't forget to see me, to create me from your own substance for I am you in your deepest self.

Simplify all your thoughts, simplify your life, your emotional claims, everything that weighs heavy on you and you will then discover the dazzling dawn of new joy. However great your suffering, in you I am the abiding sun, endless life, the wonder of the world's first morning.

With your whole heart, forgive every person from whom you feel you have not received what they should have given you. Forgive your very existence for having so wounded you.

Everything that happens to you can be offered up and transcended, transformed; it is a gift to the future of the earth. Create yourself anew constantly in that beyond of yourself which is the divine. Life is in your hands. You can make it into a golden landscape, a fairytale world.

I will come to you in whatever form you choose and that suits you but, for this to happen, be free and transparent so that I can make my way to the secret centre of your heart.

Let go of all resentment and of the slightest feeling of aversion to yourself, to anyone else or anything else.

You will see me always more alive and radiant as forgiveness heals you, and you will be able to nestle in this light-filled place where there is no loneliness.

***Question:*** *What can I do for a young friend who lives with me? She is stricken with an incurable illness and rebels against her fate.*

***He says:*** Your friend has been entrusted to you for the period of life and suffering that is given her. You can do much for her. Your loving presence is balm to her tormented soul. Don't talk too much about God now, it only makes her think of expiry dates that she cannot bear. Live life together, one moment at a time, really going into the present. Through forgetting both about the past and the future she will be able to open a door into the unknown joy that lies within, if one stops in the eternity of the present moment.

Watch the sunset with her. It can be so beautiful that one is flooded with gratitude. With your love give her the mountain that is somehow part of your own essence.

It isn't words she needs as much as a new feeling of life, a feeling that does not involve the desire to escape from her destiny. It is time she forgave herself, that she forgave life itself for its cruelty. Let go with her all the useless ties that imprison her in suffocating emotional patterns.

When her anger is exhausted and she is better able to accept her life as it now is, something very rich will be given to both of you. Don't forget to be aware of this and to reflect it. Impose nothing on her. Maturing will take place in its own time. The divine can appear somewhere else, somewhere totally unexpected. It infiltrates secretly when conscious thought has forgotten its existence.

***Question:*** *What can one do for those who have Aids? (The question is asked by someone who is involved with groups that practise visualization.)*

***He says:*** For those who have Aids and for all those separated by suffering from their inner source, the unique and absolute remedy is love.

I will suggest a visualization that can be done either in a group or alone.

Gather together in silent and peaceful joy. When you sense my presence or have reached deep relaxation, visualize those who suffer as if they were abandoned children whom one brings into the warmth of a home. Open your heart and cradle them. In love you are one with them, they are part of yourselves. Embrace this part of yourself with infinite tenderness, then entrust the sufferers to me, each one personally. At this level of relaxation you will be able to communicate with them inwardly.

You can tell those who are believers to turn their eyes to me and bathe in the ocean of my Love. You can tell those who are not that a great light keeps watch over them, the light of never-ending life. These two ways of seeing meet up beyond the mind's rigid constructions.

During the whole of the meeting be open to joy that is as clear and transparent as a mountain stream.

At other times, if you meet the sufferers, you can talk to them about what you are doing but be sensitive to their need. Don't speak of prayer to unbelievers, but of meditation or of the energy of thought. Respect each one for what he is and never impose me in any form whatever. Then I will be able to slip silently to their bedside and breathe a little light into their soul.

***Question:*** *What is the significance of Aids and is it connected in any way with the transformation we are now being called on to live?*

***He says:*** Aids shows us the extent to which we are linked and united one to another.

Like pollution, Aids is no respecter of frontiers. It is a harsh apprenticeship to unity for we are all exposed, all vulnerable—whether because of material greed (selling contaminated blood) or because of an addiction (drugs), or because of the pursuit of love (sexuality).

This disease at first allowed homosexuals to be rejected because of their difference or "fault" but now it is a threat to everyone. It makes us revise our narrow and loveless judgements, our hardened and restrictive morals.

If we do not radically transform our ways of loving, we are in danger of Aids making terrible ravages on earth.

That is perhaps the message that each Aids sufferer can give to those around him and to the world.

The disease breaks out especially in people who experience in their bodies a need to change the connection with love. This change is so radical that, up till now, death is the price.

So many musicians, artists, creative people and those of great sensitivity give their lives to make us understand this need. Their suffering cries out to us: it is time to change, to love differently.

Often people around reject them from fear, or weakness or because they refuse to open themselves to love. But often too this disease sparks off very great devotion, a heroic sharing, and a real transfiguration of feeling.

In the collective mentality Aids is a spectral presence, the ultimate threat. It is a materialization of horror that is fed by fear, and blown up by the imagination.

Let us try to look at things differently.

Obviously when you lose a child or are yourself threatened in the fulness of youth by this axe, this imminent death, it is hard to change your attitude. Detachment, however, would allow everyone and especially those with Aids to live better. They could understand that despite their misfortune, or perhaps because of it, life reveals its beauty "now" and sweeps us along in its divine momentum.

They could discover that nothing exists outside the present moment. They, more than others, are able to plunge into it totally and find the door that opens to a radiant pathway, one where the liberated soul accepts equally both living in a body and leaving it. By transmitting this discovery, lived at the price of their very existence, it becomes to others a gift of light whose impact no one is able to gauge.

From this different viewpoint, those who have not been stricken but who are afraid could perhaps tame the terrifying image they have of the disease and transform it into love.

Aids is a disease of love. It is there to teach us a different love, love that carries us to new awareness, to a different understanding of ourselves and of the universe. This new awareness knows neither rejection nor separation. It integrates the body naturally into the sacred current of life.

***Question asked by Ali:*** *I find no way out of despair.*
*(Ali is blind and wants his first name to be mentioned.)*

***He says:*** Your path in life is not the one you think it is. You wait and give way to despair, but in the depths of your heart is a jewel that you have not yet got to know. Up till now you have not recognized the inner world that can open up like a starry sky from your depths. It is not in waiting, in a desire to "do" or to "become" that you will be able to find the joy of being alive. It is not by clutching desperately at something outside yourself that you will solve your problems. It is by saying yes to the incomparable treasure of your deep being. It is by accepting what you are and what is, lovingly, that the world will reflect back to you that image of yourself, for the world is only the extension of what we ourselves are.

Perhaps you have something special to transmit, for within you lies the scorched song of the desert. This song of the desert could become the song of God or the song of Joy.

When you can allow the mystery of your being, which is full of riches, to rise from your roots, a new birth will take place in your heart. It is through plunging courageously into the night of your despair that you will be able to find the light.

***Question:*** *What can one do to alleviate suffering in the world?*

***He says:*** First of all sort out your own problems, whether they are personal or concern relationships, and find in yourself the potential for harmony and joy that you want to fill the world with. Then live these with your whole heart in adoration and gratitude.

If you can do this, or even simply work towards this state of mind, you will be able to unite yourself with the suffering of others in a loving impulse that transcends it.

Love heals suffering. It opens the doors of your soul in that place where bliss alone is possible. You then relieve suffering because you are on a different level and let yourself be guided intuitively to those who have chosen you as a mirror to free themselves from it. Your gestures become quite naturally those of penetrating and welcome compassion.

In drawing closer to unity, you notice that all sufferings merge, whatever their origin. When a child cries somewhere, crushed by despair, it is you who weep in him, but at the same time it is the pain of all children on earth weeping in you.

When an abandoned dog waits for its master till it dies, it is you who have been abandoned, but at the same time you live the great pain of abandonment all down the ages.

When you become aware of the unity of suffering, you become aware of the unity of life and you are no longer separate from others. It does not mean identifying sentimentally with the other, for in such identification you are still held in the grip of the ego. It here means a change of awareness that modifies something on the planet: you become able to transform your own suffering, as well as the world's, into an offering, into "seeing it differently", seeing it as part of a vaster whole. You begin to discover the joy that underlies all suffering, and your viewpoint changes. You see both sides of the coin at once, because all suffering that is accepted, lived and transcended can become joy or serenity. This joy is then transmitted from heart to heart like a cry of release.

You can also see that transcending suffering, in fact the ego, gives birth to joy.

If mankind stops losing contact with its divine essence, in other words with the unity of life, it will no longer be necessary to suffer.

Life's journey can then take on the sparkling colours of returning to its origins, to the undivided bliss lying dormant in our hearts.

We dread the world coming to an end, yet that end could become an awakening, giving birth to the radiant and solar power of Love.

***Question:*** *I want to control my actions. I don't succeed and it makes me very unhappy. What must I do?*

***He says:*** Lift your eyes to me. I am your Source and your happiness. I give you my Love. Look at it. It fills you with light. It is tender and limitless. Why hate yourself when I, Jesus, love you?

Forget the beliefs that forge an image of you as being unworthy and guilty. You are imprisonned in the narrow channels of a morality that cuts you to pieces.

By loving yourself deep down you are loving me, for you are not separate either from me or from others.

Look at me and the walls you build to torture yourself with will collapse in a great shout of joy.

Seek in yourself the life blood that lets you laugh and shake off the jumble of your negative thoughts. They ruin the beauty of every step you take on the earth.

If you could but allow yourself to see me and let the spark of my presence rise up in your heart, you would know that my Love is so great it asks you for nothing.

Accept the right to be your full self and live in the wonderful light of happiness you have always refused.

You are allowed to be happy; you are allowed to eat, even to eat too much.

Escape from the patterns you impose on yourself. One side of you assumes power and makes the other side submit, so that these bits of you fight and divide you.

There is no sin, it is only division that leads to suffering.

Look clearly, and with amused love at everything you spurn in yourself.

The bits you reject are just abandoned children. Take them into your heart and cradle them tenderly. This will help you to give up all judgement and find unity again. By accepting what you are, without trying to be anything else, you will get rid of illusion and the mutation can take place from within. Then you will find me, for I am "one" with every living cell of the universe.

***Question:*** *Can one avoid suffering and so deflect the course of one's karma?*

***He says:*** If you believe in karma, that means in the restoration of a balance as regards past actions, you cannot avoid suffering. But by letting go of that belief, and transforming your view of yourself and the world, you can discover another level of consciousness. At this other level you are free of all suffering because the joy of your discovery is of greater importance than the horizontal plane of events in your everyday life.

The keys to changing your view of yourself and the world could be surrender and offering.

Let go of your mental constructs, free your spirit of everything that weighs on it, and find in yourself the pulse of life that offers such expressions of the ego and attachments to something higher. Those ideas and prejudices, the expectations and desire for security all spring from that same ego and those same attachments. If you can offer them up and let them dissolve in the other way of being, you will catch sight of the unknown shores of a land of freedom, a new land that is not divided. If you can shed useless baggage as you go along, you will find your true nature, divine nature, in the depths of your heart. It is the current of light that links you to the stars, it is the shout of release, the song of Love that is without beginning or end. If you can merge with this ocean of beauty, you will see that death, suffering and fear are no more than a distant memory, a dance of shadows, a pathetic ballet without reality.

***Question:*** *What can I do to get over a moral ordeal that has resulted from physical suffering? How can I recover my energy?*

***He says:*** The moral ordeal that you are living through because of physical difficulties can be resolved swiftly.

Go into yourself and with great attention examine the problems you have experienced in life. Bring these problems to the surface again, and plunge into them with your whole being so that there is no space between them and you. Bring them into the unity of your being. Love them completely so that they no longer divide you. Guilt hollows out a space between you and you. The two sides are at war without your even being aware of it. This guilt forces you to pay in some way and your physical difficulties represent the price.

Accept that you are what you are and have been what you were. Put all this into the arms of Love, into the fire of life that burns up all problems, even those of guilt.

Don't judge what you have done in life. Your experiences have made you evolve. Thank them for bringing you where you now are. Let go of any notion of control and make a gift of your destiny to the divine that guides you. In this gift you will find strength and healing.

It is thanks to it too that you will go through the door of a new reality.

***Question:*** *I feel guilty because I didn't answer the call of my inner voice and my life is now nothing but suffering. How can I find a way out of this hell?*

***He says:*** Give me your guilt. No blame weighs on your shoulders.

You have strayed into a world that doesn't suit you, for it does not have the transparency of Love.

The experience of light is what does suit you. You will recognize it because it brings joy, serenity, true inner liberty and love for oneself as much as for others. Experiencing this transforms your everyday life and gives it harmony. Each of your actions then becomes a note of music in the symphony of life.

It would be better for you now to move into a more rational world where you could find the usual forms of psychological security. A certain vulnerability has let entities infiltrate in order to deceive you.

So it is by immersing yourself in practical reality that you will find strong roots again. From them you can let the tree of joy grow.

Regret nothing. I, Jesus, the light of your heart, love you unconditionally. You will find me quite simply by the roadside. One day, in the silence, you will see the spring that gushes out and will know it is my smile that floods you. There is nothing to search for, nothing to do, just open your hands and let my love join you.

Go calmly about finding earthly tasks that call for creativity. You can create works of art, or a garden or simply turn the present moment into a moment of fulfilment, a moment when laughter shows you the blessings of life on earth and the reassuring threshold of your home.

You are incarnate here on earth and it is by starting from this basic reality that I can grow in you.

***Question:*** *Why am I unhappy?*

***He says:*** Your difficulty with life is like wearing too heavy a coat that weighs you down. You can take it off. Simply give up the ideas that shut you into compartments and divide you. The whole of life passes through you and you are an intermediary for the beauty of the world. See it by just removing the labels that say "you must" do this or that. Nothing more is asked of you than to be happy. Let go of all concepts that confine you to one way of thinking or another. Let the sweetness of being alive flow through your body, through your mind and your soul, whatever meaning you may attach to that word.

Find in yourself the silence of the depths into which disappears the desire to have or to be anything other than what you are. In that silence is born the constantly renewed wonder of being alive. And also from that silence you will draw the incomparable riches that are in you and that you have not yet exploited. At that level, every gesture you make will be true and lead on to the next. Then you will walk in the calm happiness destined for you.

If you let go of your will to "get a grip" on the world, if you open your hands and do not cling to anything—whether goods, affections or even certainties—a completely new splendour will come back to you. This splendour far surpasses anything you can imagine, if you can accept the transformation and the unknown it entails.

Through understanding that it is enough just to be alive and let life's smile flow in you, you will come into contact with absolute joy and, from all sides, the world will send back to you that reflection of yourself.

***Question:*** *What can one do when torn between one's family and a new love?*

***He says:*** The events life brings you have a meaning that is not always obvious at first sight. Everything given you, whether joy or suffering, can be the means of your transformation. Don't think of your situation as intolerable. Don't place it in duality: what must I do, must I obey my moral code or my heart's desire?

Change the elements of the problem and look for the meaning of this new encounter and of the situation into which you are plunged. Don't refuse suffering. When suffering is lived fully, when it is accepted and transcended, other horizons are revealed, and other levels of awareness can be reached.

When you transform yourself in this way you help all those around you. A situation is unconsciously "needed" by all those involved as each person is called to evolve one way or another through it. It is not easy to look at one's life this way when plunged into the problem. But little by little some of the way ahead lights up and shows you that you are always accompanied, even if you didn't know it. You find everything that happens to you has a very precise meaning in the design of your life as a whole and includes a positive aspect. We are all called, each in our own way, to discover another form of love, one that asks for nothing and where the gift of self constitutes the most complete joy. This form of love can never be unfair to anyone because it possesses neither anything nor anyone. It is rare for human love not to be marred by power or possessiveness and yet, if it is sincere, in it there is always found a spark of divine love. By making that spark in oneself grow no other problem can arise, or rather problems are burnt up as and when they do arise. Then they become the unknown flame that changes your outlook and you are born into a different world.

***Question:*** *I have lost the use of my legs and doctors can do nothing for me. At the same time I am living an extraordinary experience of the Divine Presence. I do not understand the reason for my illness.*

***He says:*** There is a deep division between this experience and the narrow and strict religion of your childhood. You cannot undo its hold over you and so cannot fully accept the new experience. By understanding this not only with your mind but also with the whole of your being, you take the first step towards your healing. Let yourself be filled more and more by your experience, live it without reference to anything else and you will recover the use of your legs.

Your ardent and thirsty soul is held in check by concepts from the past that prevent your whole self from being expressed. These concepts feed a huge sense of guilt about what is happening to you: guilt so powerful and deep-seated that it throws you off balance to the extent of making you lose the use of your legs.

This duality goes back a long way, for while you were still very young part of you revolted against the rigid side of your religion.

When you are strong enough to "stand on your own feet" without the security that the Church represents, you will be able to use your legs again normally.

But as there is meaning in everything that happens, it is the suffering and illness, once you were able to accept them, that have given you the opportunity to go beyond them in this transcendence of yourself, which means the experience of the divine.

When you have found your inner unity, nothing will prevent you staying in the Church, but your relationship to it will no longer be one of dependence or guilt.

***Question:*** *Must one get to know the roots of one's fear in order to free oneself from it?*

***He says:*** Fear is like a vast invisible creeping plant that reaches into each nerve, each fibre of your body. It feeds on the flicker of a thought, on the slightest criticism, or the most insignificant everyday incident. One needs to know where its roots lie so as to stop feeding it. Approach it one step at a time, integrate it completely with your being without rejecting it, take it into your arms like a small unhappy child, and eventually it will yield its secret. Love can dissolve this troublesome parasite. The more it is refused and separated, ignored or buried, the stronger it grows. But when it is brought into the unity of your love, it loses its grim aspect. This first approach can be swift and at a stroke fear will be burnt up in joy's great fire. But another approach is possible, and that involves becoming aware of oneself.

For instance, a gnawing fear of death torments you. What does this fear say? It says I do not wish to disappear. Who says "I"? Your ego says "I", the side of you that is nothing but illusion, the side of you that surrounds itself with protections, with ramparts, and hardens itself to keep intact its arrogance and self-importance. When you notice this ego and its contortions, you can't help laughing at it. It hates laughter, for that deflates it.

When laughter and a clear view of your ego have shown up its little ploys, you will see how closely it is linked to the fear of death. But the side of you that is flame or spirit, and actually is a grain of the absolute, does not fear death because it knows itself to be universal and immortal.

Once you have recognized your ego and its various ruses, you meet another aspect of yourself. In this aspect no fear can exist, because it is the wonderful current of life. The current flows on and on, renewing itself to infinity.

On the journey to self-awareness, this is how to go through different stages. First you make contact with your mechanisms, dismantle their deeply hidden springs and discover, with the clarity of an open mind, your secret workings. This calls for courage and total absence of judgement. Only then will your essential being unveil itself in its most dazzling truth.

***Question:*** *How should I view my suffering and illness?*
*(Question asked by someone very ill who suffers greatly.)*

***He says:*** It is by consciously accepting suffering and giving up all resistance, in fact by going beyond the frontiers of fear and of the body, that you will understand the reason for your illness better. You will see it as a cry from your depths, an expression of your own inner demand.

Transcendence is being asked of you because it is what you hope for. Suffering can lead you there if you take it into your heart and offer it up. Offering it up means offering it to Love.

When you accept suffering completely, it is transformed into the pure diamond of what you are deep down. When you are united with it, you abandon yourself to Love and let the layers of illusion that conceal the core of your being fall away. Each person chooses their path to the light. But it is always through love you reach it, even through loving your own suffering: that alone can help you to transcend it.

Trust in your destiny, but also in your freedom, freedom to transform shadow into light solely by the strength of your look at yourself and the world.

Carry on peacefully. I am the door in you that opens onto the infinite and I hold your hands through all that happens to you. Look at me. Already you will see breaking, beyond the storm, the sunlit treasure of dawn.

***Question:*** *Why is there suffering?*

***He says:*** Suffering seems inevitable in the illusory world of duality, but it is only inevitable if the ego buries itself in it. It is never anything but the expression of separation (or the illusion of separation). Whenever one traces any type of suffering to its source, one senses this separation and at the same time a longing for unity. Suffering therefore, when it is fully lived and transcended, allows one to become conscious of this longing for unity. It spurs us on to set about dismantling its mechanism. For in fact suffering is not necessary. It only arises when lack of thought makes us blind. It is a lifeline thrown out to show us our prison, our conditioning, our illusions, our judgements or the straitjacket of our aversions, in fact all the things that chop us up.

When one traces the course of suffering back to its origins, and so lives the duality completely, it becomes part of the primordial paradox for it can change its register and be experienced as a joy that frees one precisely from time and from duality.

Physical suffering belongs to this paradox. It stems from our absent-mindedness, from our inability to see our restricting constructions, our ties. Illnesses are often the tangible result of an unconscious refusal to leave our cage, for it is under the illusion of protecting oneself that one most surely suffocates.

All ties are aspects of suffering, whether they are emotional, material, intellectual or spiritual. One can also be tied to ideas, ideas about what one ought to be or what others ought to be or do, and so on.

Through becoming aware of the nature of our ties and the fact that they separate us, we transform suffering and draw closer to the natural movement of life. In the pulsation of the universe, no suffering is possible.

## Chapter Five

# Death

*Message to someone who is dying and has no fear of death, abandoning himself to the image of his faith.*

***He says:*** Infinite light keeps watch over you. Your eyes are already turned towards it and a thousand golden shafts sparkle in your thoughts. Go confidently to your fulfilment.

I, Jesus, take you in my arms. No burden whatever still weighs on you. You are free to take flight for your transparent soul has shed earth's heaviness. You have fulfilled the destiny of your inmost being with ardour and are flooded with grace.

Thus I map out your path and you walk with me in the footsteps of joy.

***Question:*** *How is it possible for joy to filter through the idea of death?*

***He says:*** True joy is an expression of freedom, meaning that fear has disappeared, especially the fear of death, whether fear of your own death or that of others.

If you are no longer subject to this basic fear, you can live your joy fully, without constraint. But in order not to fear death, you need to sense deep in your cells that life has no end and that death, except for external appearances, is a mental image lacking reality. The feeling of "being" that you live through your body at the moment doesn't disappear. On the contrary, you can imagine that this connected part of you, this endlessly renewed joy, has a correspondence in your physical body.

Make contact with this most alive part, the part that cannot disappear and is all the more real for being less tangible.

In these conditions, the passage from life to death can be nothing other than sparkling joy.

Death comes as a gift and release to all when you no longer depend on external appearances but have "entered" that other part of yourself.

It is by going into that part that you change your level of awareness. There, death is constantly present and the joy of rebirth cannot be separated from it.

Joy and suffering, death and rebirth are the inescapable aspects of our existence.

On the horizontal level of duality, we dissociate them, but each time we are in contact with the divine that dwells in us, no dissociation is possible.

*Message to someone very ill, who is terrified of death.*

***He says:*** I am close to you at every moment. You are my small child and your hand is in mine. Forget fear.

Nothing will happen to you. If I take you on a journey, I promise you the luminous journey of Love. On it you will find your own splendour and fulfilment. Hand over your anxiety to me, hand over your future, your worries and your heavy thoughts. If you give me all that, I will turn it into light and you will be weightless in the arms of the infinite.

Let yourself be carried. Can't you see I weep at not being able to join you? Open your hands and your home to me, open your heart to me. I wait patiently for you to want to find me, because I am the solution to your torments. I transform fear into pearls of joy, suffering into unexpected and marvellous gifts. In you, I am the ferment of happiness and eternity, I am your unfailing and secret support.

Be willing to see me, to be reborn different in me so that you discover at last that life is never-ending and leads us joyfully to suns of unforeseeable beauty.

*Message for a dying woman.*

***He says:*** Don't worry, simply let yourself be carried by these arms of light that never leave you. They belong to the image of the Love you dream of in your deepest self. Let yourself bathe in acceptance of whatever happens to you. You are wholly ready for transformation. This transformation will lead you to a place whose splendour you cannot imagine. Let go of all the refusals that still belong to a particular way of looking at things. There are no grounds for punishing you. You have committed no sin. Sin is simply a construct of the mind.

You are free, spread your wings, soar with the current of joy that seeks only to lift you beyond yourself.

The time for suffering is over. Accept this great happiness: to know that Love is all-powerful, that one has only to abandon oneself to it to be transformed and transform the world.

***Question:*** *How, under the most favourable conditions, should we prepare ourselves for the transition of death?*

***He says:*** During life, the most important preparation for death is to be constantly in touch with what transcends us.

If we let the living flame of the divine grow in us, if we keep its luminous presence constantly in mind, we will be able to invoke it naturally at the moment of death.

This calls for practice and for constant attention, but the practice also leads to discovering the secret movement that links us to the events in our lives, and to the underlying motivation of their unfolding. All that seemed to be madness, absurdity or useless suffering takes on meaning and has its justification.

In our daily life, attention to our "inner being" teaches us to cut down on useless chatter, whether it is shared with others or confined to the reservoir of an overexcited brain. Noise and activity distract and blind us. They show up the fear that hides us from ourselves and prevents our divine spark from appearing.

Paradoxically, to prepare for death in this way allows life to blossom in new serenity. Then one can see that death isn't an end, but could be a birth, a change of state that meets up with the spark and is wholly absorbed into it.

So what is suggested in this progress to the infinite that is always beginning again, is that in a single impulse we offer up both these wonderful journeys, one of life and the other of death, without separating them. The flame we have nurtured in life draws them together and unifies them.

Once one starts paying attention to one's inner light, it becomes increasingly clear that death has no effect on the existence of the divine in us. So death no longer has any reality, apart from what we choose to give it. It is enough to look at it differently and throw another light on it to defuse its power over our imagination. It is possible to get rid of the fear, the fascination and the rejection that we project onto it.

Let us discover that life and death are indivisibly beautiful and in harmony with the great rhythms of the cosmos. In truth, they are revealed in the throb of the universe, in those immense pulsations that echo from world to world and from space to space.

Life and death are met with at every level of being and manifestation, from the minutest insect to the song of the stars.

Life and death express transformation and diversity, and also what we actually are, that is to say the Dance or the Laughter of God.

## Chapter Six

# Art

***Question:*** *What is the spiritual message of Memling's triptych "The mystical marriage of Saint Catherine" and how can one communicate it to an audience?*

**He says:** The spiritual message of this painting is a vision of the painter's expressed through the painting itself, not through the words one could add to it. The painter sensed at great depth the inner vision of Catherine of Sienna and her spiritual union, but the scene that is represented can be looked at from many different levels. First there is the anecdotal level, then the symbolic, and lastly the level that touches a more secret sphere, where the painter communicates silently with the mystical experience of Saint Catherine. At this level, words can never be anything but a veil drawn over a different reality, one which cannot be expressed in any language except that of the painting itself.

To communicate this message to an audience, it should be enough to exhibit the work of art and to be deeply in communion with it oneself. But every person understands in their own way. Some find the colour, the beauty of the faces, or the great complexity of the composition are what speak to them. Others are moved on a different plane: something touches them, but they don't know what. Still others analyse each detail and are reassured if they can compare or refer the details to something with which they are already familiar. And for some, the painting itself opens up in them a yearning for different horizons. But can one describe the mystery of art? It has so many facets that it is very difficult to pin down in categories. Each picture can communicate in a thousand different ways and often the story told in images is but the clothing for an inspiration whose origin the artist himself does not know.

***Question:*** *Should I take up studying the cello?*

**He says:** For you, study of the cello is the golden bough on which your happiness rests. Don't hesitate. Music will allow you to give expression to the rather sombre world in which you shut yourself and through expressing it, doors will open to different clarities. It will also provide you with a bridge to others.

Don't, however, place too much weight on striving for perfection "to please others". Play for yourself first of all and through playing as well as possible for yourself, that means as close as you can to the country of your heart, you will draw nearer to others.

Don't forget the paths of joy: they are filled with music. Rejoice if you can undertake these studies. They might suit you far better than you think.

In the times that are coming we will have increasing need of voices or ways that guide us beyond ourselves, towards unknown lands. In deciding to take up these studies you have set your foot on the first step of a new stage. The steps that you take on this path could correspond to the direction of your future vocation, not only through interpreting the works of others, but above all with regard to a different form of communication. This communication would be in the realm of transmitting a new way of being and of thinking.

Be confident and keep listening to your inner melody. It guides you and never leaves you.

***Question:*** *What part does music have to play in our connection with the divine?*

**He says:** Music is the divine channel par excellence. It leads us on the luminous current that links us to a different intelligence, the intelligence of the heart.

Of course this opening to a different space is a personal opening, and corresponds to the meeting of two sensibilities—the creator's and the listener's. But music also embodies the collective aspirations of an era.

This is true of all the arts. They are never anything but the reflection of our desires for something that transcends us and sometimes they express the most secret aspects of those desires.

At this time of transformation, music can be a means of launching us towards the unknown of a new era. At present our aspiration is for the survival of the planet. It is a straightforward and essential aspiration. Music is the gift that allows us to express our transcendence and materialize a desire shared by the whole of humanity.

Sound is a key that can open the door of the divine in ourselves and let it spread rapidly.

The time has passed for exploiting music as an intellectual pursuit or an eccentric game aimed at an "elite". Music is a royal means to appeal, to open and to find release.

The threat of extinction broods more or less consciously in mankind's heart. Its menace at last gathers us into a common goal that we could achieve if we found unity with our own "being", with others and with the universe.

If music can transmit this vital aspiration, it will itself become the intelligence of Love.

## Chapter Seven

# Spirituality

***Question:*** *What should I do when people want me to be their guide?*

***He says:*** You cannot prevent people from wanting you to be their guide, but don't ever think of this role as having any importance, for the ego gets hold of it very quickly and skilfully. You are all one another's guides. If, at one moment, you are someone's "master", the next moment that person can be yours.

Great vigilance is needed to avoid any bond of dominant/dominated starting up. The dominant one's ego inflates and the dominated one lives by proxy. No evolution can take place where a relationship of power and submission exists, at any rate on the level of that relationship.

Empathy and compassion never lead either to judgement or to relationships of power.

Be a living flame whose radiance can sometimes set alight the inner flame of those who are ready. This is the way for you to be a guide.

***Question:*** *How can I rid myself of what still hinders my inner evolution?*

***He says:*** Go into yourself, into your unfathomable depths. To do this eliminate stress and all the interferences of thought or will that emanate from the part of you that is not yet integrated.

When you are in the stillness of that great peace, you will be able to cast off your moorings at a stroke. That is where you will be able to transform yourself wholly. New springtime shoots will then push through. By letting go of all desire to be different or to change others at this deep level, it will be your own transformation that transmits itself. Then you will know exactly what to do, for your actions will stem from the root of your being and will not result from any duality such as: "I want to help Y. to change, to recover"—which implies a division between oneself and the other.

By starting from the basic acceptance of "what is", transformation can take place. You will then discover not only that the surge of light going through you does so on its own, but also that it reaches you through others.

Out of saying "Yes, I let go the grip of my will on the world" a seed can come to life. This seed will grow and act with the dazzling power of Love. At that moment no desire whatever will disturb your inner peace. You will understand this language because you are destined to go through this mutation.

***Question:*** *How can I regain the bliss of a spiritual experience I once had but that has not happened again?*

***He says:*** My presence is in your heart, not in your head, and whenever you go down into your heart you find me there, for I never leave you. When you least expect it, when you haven't prepared anything, when you simply open your hands, I can fill you with light so completely that my look passes through your eyes.

Let this light shine in you. Don't decide how events ought to take place. Don't try to relive something that you have already lived. You can't capture me, I am the freest spark of yourself. Abandon yourself like a small child to the immense love that is given you. Through understanding that you are accepted totally, just as you are, you will once again find unity in your heart.

The sense of unity, always alive and varied, will be given you "differently". Don't fail to recognize it.

***Author's Question:*** *Is there anything special I should do to help on or speed up my transformation for it to accord with a more general transformation?*

***He says:*** Contemplate your happiness with all the simplicity and openness you are capable of. This is the only "experience" I am asking you to live. You don't have to tie yourself in knots to try out some exotic transformation. That would mean you were referring to certain experiences described in books, whether contemporary or past, from here or elsewhere.

The transformation takes place on its own. It settles in without your actually being aware of it. It blends in with your own way, which is harmonious and quiet. It is by keeping your eyes on your Beloved that you activate happiness on earth. Never lose sight of him either in yourself or everywhere else, for he teaches you the limitless Love that dissolves you in unity.

Hug the flame of divine Love close to you. It is an earthly happiness, though it is not of this world. It is a joy that hovers on the edge of the impossible and yet takes root, more solid than rock, at the heart of your reality.

Sometimes you seem to feel you ought to leap into the void, and an old fear resurfaces. So why fix on the idea that one "ought" to leap into the void? There is no "ought". Stay open and clear, ready to welcome me in any shape or form and you will walk effortlessly in the steps of eternity.

***Question:*** *How can I really be myself?*

***He says:*** Connect yourself to the infinitude of my Presence without fear. There you will find tender and absolute joy that entails no duty. Turn your eyes to the highest light, then your hands will open of their own accord and the gifts life has destined for you will pour out naturally. They will come to life in your heart and you will need to do nothing more than let them flower. In this way fresh inspiration will constantly take wing from you, expressing the essence of what you are.

Forget the stress and irritation that keep you in intermediate zones where I cannot join you. It is in these zones that certain entities can insinuate themselves and slip past your guard. Those entities are the result of the anxieties and desires for domination that people project, either on others or on themselves. They confront you with your own dividedness.

Let the shimmering river of existence flow in you. Don't cling to the idea that one "must" do one thing rather than another. Don't seize hold of life, let it follow its own path. If you allow yourself to be guided you will understand that you yourself are that bit of life which passes and never ends.

***Question:*** *Does God love his creation which goes from innocence (the Son) to illusion-division; from the knowledge of unity to imaginary scattering?*

***He says:*** The All, the Unity, or God if that name suits you, recognizes himself in every manifestation. He loves himself in each of the droplets of life in the universe. He is realized in them. He amuses himself to infinity with his creation and becomes aware of himself through it. He is amused too by those bits of him that consider themselves to be separate. He "sees" himself in all things in the same way that each thing can be reflected in him. In this vast game of mirrors, when the bit that thinks itself separated finds the level of unity once again, it becomes "Creator" while also being "creature". This means that each morsel of life on the earth and elsewhere constitutes the possibility of infinite creation. The All creates himself in creating each of his parts and each of his parts creates him when it plays the game of non-duality, that is to say when it becomes aware of its source.

The "innocent Son", if he represents a manifestation

that is not part of the illusion of being separated, draws towards knowledge or co-creation those who are ready for it.

For you, in the middle, the seer who asks an intellectual and metaphysical question of this order, the answer can only be couched in terms of the same order. But another reality is possible which does not belong to that category. It is found in the disappearance of all speculative thought. No words can convey it. It is lived. Therefore it is very difficult to establish contact between reason, which is concerned with manipulating concepts, and this other reality. The intellect can circle round without ever being able to grasp it. The only way for the intellect to make contact is for it to scuttle itself. Intellectual speculation can be useful to the extent that it is able to come to a halt in the silence and give itself up. It has reached the end of its journey and the birth of something else.

When man's limited intelligence abandons itself to the unknown of another intelligence, when it is no longer imprisoned by particular concepts or ways of thinking, it is possible to reach this reality that can be sensed but is not contained in words. Then there is a splendid and faceless explosion, the fire of life bursts out, the shout of freedom, the infinite spiral that renews and perpetuates itself without beginning or end.

But, once again, how can one draw closer with words to this "inconceivable", born out of silence and a leap into the unknown?

***Question:*** *How can I neither stray into idolatry nor deviate from accepted teaching if I give in to the attraction B. has for me?*

***He says:*** The divine is everywhere, in B. just as it is in you. Why split it up? You have every right, complete freedom to recognize it wherever you want to recognize it. Idolatry can only be conceived of in relation to the ego, in relation to a power of separation. B. is not someone different from yourself. Like you, he is life, but he is wholly life and no longer an individual, because he has no ego, no boundaries. Having said that, all paths are good that lead you to the inner truth that suits you right now. You cannot go astray if you are true to yourself (this means that thinking, speaking, doing and living are all of a piece).

Today, you need the reassuring limits of traditional teaching. It is helpful and right for you at this moment. Tomorrow you may perhaps want to be part of the fairy tale that B. offers. The day after tomorrow, a new upsurge might fill you wholly and you would then find the universal Source in your own heart. Let the truth move in accordance with what you are at the moment. Be willing to change, to slip into the ever fresh movement of life. Your truth will take on the colours of the rainbow. It will modulate itself in accordance with your sensitivity and the evolution of your being. It will play like a light breeze on the joyous ship of your destiny. Navigate fearlessly, unfurling your sails to the wind of the open sea, and as your days and your nights go by, nothing will be able to prevent you living the silent, dazzling, light of the divine.

***Question:*** *What should one do when an inner search distances one from the rest of the family?*

***He says:*** The path towards the divine is solitary and silent. Each one finds it in their own way and the only possible way to share it is to reflect it in one's actions, one's thoughts and the openness of one's heart.

Sometimes it is hard to find the divine in one's daily life, and yet the two are not separated. One doesn't have to switch off from the practical world to find it, but on the contrary to go into that world with one's whole being to discover, beyond appearances, a different breath, the breath of the underlying unity that links all things together.

If one feels distanced from one's partner or family on account of this kind of search, it is because one is passing judgement on the others: they ought to change, they should follow the same path or the same sort of search, it would help them so much, and so on. But this judgement is already a lack of love and an obstacle to the evolution that has started. We have nothing to impose on others, either as regards our beliefs, or the way we live. Each person finds their path when they are truly themselves and free of all constraint. No one else could know in what way and by what means they will find the inner space that brings joy and freedom. Talks or so-called "spiritual" exercises are rarely the ferment of discovery, especially for those who prefer windsurfing or watercolour painting. These talks and exercises are then felt to be a reproach and weigh on the harmony and stability of a family.

Walk calmly towards your inner sun. Your tact, your

ardour and radiance will be the surest guarantees of joy and serenity both for you and for those around you. Then you will transmit, without even being aware of it, that inestimable gift, the light of your heart.

***Question:*** *Why do negative reactions surface when I make contact with B.? Why am I sent vague or disagreeable dreams? Nevertheless, I would like to think of him as a supreme manifestation.*

***He says:*** B. manifests himself in each person not only through what they feel about themselves, but also through their problems which come to the surface. For example, if fear of authority, of power or of something else is present in you, B. will also manifest himself through that.

He often says: "I am yourselves". For many people, he is an image of the divine in a human being, but he has no reality as an individual because he has no ego.

If he manifests himself to you negatively, examine very deeply and clearly the fear or the guilt that is in you. He could represent some authority that you judge or regret as you feel it to be an integral part of yourself. Perhaps fear still exists in you that dates back to lack of understanding from your father or mother, and B. faces you with this fear so that you can overcome it.

It is possible that you refuse to accept in yourself the power we all have that could make us reach unknown worlds.

To sum up, fear of authority and fear of the unknown perhaps lie behind your negative impression. Accept calmly what is given you without placing too much importance on it. Perhaps the manifestations will change as you come to understand your own mechanisms better. It isn't essential for you to adopt B. as the model of supreme manifestation. You can adopt a different image, or no image at all. In that case you keep a spark of light in your heart and all the supports, the images or the concepts fade away.

Before knowing what suits you best, however, get to know the deep motives behind your actions and thoughts. Uncover and bring to the light all the impulses you have stowed away in your unconscious. Then you will find it increasingly easy to free yourself of the little discords that mar the constant fulfilment of your happiness. If you can clarify your awareness of yourself, and make it into an ever more radiant work of art, you will be led quite naturally to new landscapes whose beauty you cannot imagine.

***Question:*** *What is the difference between the soul and the spirit?*

***He says:*** Your soul is your personal journey this side of God. That is to say from the side of a movement of transformation aimed at refining your ability to sense the divine ever more keenly.

Your spirit is not personal, it is that other movement of yourself linked to the pulse of life. In general terms therefore it is the life force, but when it expresses itself through your limitations, it explodes them.

***Question:*** *What is my mission in this life?*

***He says:*** Your mission is the slow maturing taking place in your soul of which you are not always aware.

Your mission is the surrender that sometimes floods you and opens you to contact with divine space, the space where my Love fills you. Your mission is to let your barriers, your agitation and your anxieties all fall away, so that I can express myself through you. Your mission is forgiveness. Forgive yourself as I forgive you and as you forgive others. Your mission is to go into your heart, into the peaceful garden where I keep watch over you.

Give me each day, witholding nothing of your anxiety or your guilt, in the same way that each day you spread your generosity on those around you.

Your life is successful for your have met me, not through dogma or duty, but in the reality of your heart and your everyday life.

***Question:*** *How can one keep to the right path, and what does the right path mean?*

***He says:*** The right path is the current of life, that is to say the course that leads to harmony in every gesture, every thought, every action relating to oneself, to others and to the universe.

When one's being is tuned like a violin, it plays "true". Perhaps this is one of the reasons for our time on earth. Whenever a screech is produced, we become aware of the need to tune the instrument that we are.

External events often send us back to the problems we still need to sort out. They are therefore the measure of what is going on in us. Looked at like this, they take on a new aspect. This changed aspect is in itself a transformation. It sheds a different light on all life's problems, for it sees why they are necessary. It sees that without them understanding is not possible. It allows for an expansion of awareness and an acceptance of events whatever they might be.

Whenever you are upset by what takes place, examine carefully the resonance that is set off. Look at the significance the event could have for your emotional and mental workings, or for your inner evolution.

Once you can decipher the meaning of either happy or unhappy situations as they affect your personal development, you will be a well-tuned violin and your destiny will fit into other perspectives. Your path will be "true", you will be able to play your life's tune in the rhythm that suits you. And you will see that this rhythm also suits those close to you, as well as the song of the earth, then that of the stars and the whole universe.

***Question:*** *How can I find the unconditional Love I dream of? Is suffering necessary to achieve it?*

***He says:*** You set your aspiration very high and it is suffering lived through and transcended that shows you the measure of such an aspiration.

The unconditional Love you dream of is the setting free of each moment. It corresponds to sparkling and endlessly renewed joy. Look clearly at what your suffering centres on, in other words, what you are attached to. If you can live your relationships in love and not because of attachments, you will have no problems. Be very aware of your deep motivations and distinguish between those that derive from the ego and those that stem from your inner light. The ego is always involved in power and attachment.

All conflicts arise from attachment to an idea, a moral code, a way of behaving, a possession, a memory, a person, etc. Don't rely blindly on social or religious precepts. Find in yourself the secret truth that connects you to the divine. It won't necessarily conform to conventional patterns. Discover the free and wild space in which you can open your heart to the whole universe and be truly yourself.

You long for the fervour that knows no limits, yet fear the side of you that wants to catch fire. Never forget that the divine breath is a flame of joy and love. Burn up in it everything that obstructs you, everything that does not come from the secret truth that is yours alone.

You are close to crossing the river. Dare to change your way of looking, and the world will change its face. A country of wonders will spring from your heart, a country of light where nothing whatsoever is separate.

***Question:*** *Is it possible to be wholly in the present yet at the same time aware of all that goes on in oneself?*

***He says:*** To be aware of all that goes on in oneself is precisely to live wholly in the present. However this does not concern an analysis stemming from the mind and the ego, but the neutral look that could be called the look of one's inner light.

Because this inner light is the link between all things, it allows the ego to dissolve in the whole, at least during such moments of silent and uncompromising observation as come from a different "consciousness".

So it is not a matter of listing every action, emotion, thought or sensation but of slipping them into the alchemical crucible of that other look. It is precisely in the all-embracing look which is Love's that thought can be transformed so that it is no longer a storehouse of useless memories distorting the encounter with oneself.

If you observe the unfolding of your inner life in this way, you are as "at one" with it as when you gaze at a rose and could melt into its scent and beauty.

When thought is fed by judgements, by the need to classify, by a heavy load of learning and outdated memories, it is not possible to enter the present.

Be free of the past, and released from your projections about the future. That is the surest way you can truly penetrate into the self and into the present—the eternal cradle of renewal. Then there will no longer be any difference between the endless observation of life and you yourself who give expression to it.

To be aware of what goes on in oneself means to be aware of the whole ocean and not of each single drop of water in it.

This is the sense in which this realization corresponds to the infinite present where time and space dissolve.

***Question:*** *Where does one draw spiritual energy from that is more than just courage to exist?*

***He says:*** Spiritual energy never leaves us. It is life itself.

On the level of duality we are separated from it because we are unable to let ourselves slip into the current of life. We don't accept the possibility of saying "yes" to what happens consciously and actively.

The will for separateness that makes us try and control every situation shuts us into a prison we do not see. By letting go one's grip at every instant, spiritual energy can be endlessly renewed. Acceptance hollows out the present moment till it becomes infinite space. Time then vanishes in what might be called "the presence" or the divine breath. In this different way of existing the spring gushes forth. Not only does it gush forth, but we realize we are the spring itself. This observation transforms us. It leads us to a state that allows the energy of life to be activated, to be passed on like an echo and to be expressed in its flowering.

***Question:*** *What is the root of doubt? And what is the surest way of uprooting it?*

***He says:*** Doubt is born in what divides us, that means the ego. Like the ego, doubt is necessary at a certain level of being. It presides over all the choices of earthly life. It weighs up the pros and cons. It acts as the measure, the scales of everyday life. It makes one reflect, avoid mistakes, illusion, deception, pretences, and by successive eliminations can lead to a different level of being.

But once this level has been reached, once the illusion of duality has dissolved, doubt becomes a hindrance, a black sail on the horizon. It prevents the emergence of the divine, the fusion with light, because now it is generated by another side of the ego: fear of the unknown. It is one's fear of setting off on a journey of the soul, imagined as an unbearable desert, as loss of identity. Doubt tempts one to renounce the light. It pursues, torments, insists, insinuates itself and merges with the little me that is always full of fear.

The surest way to disempower it is to look at it tenderly, and to cradle it in one's heart and in the unity of Love.

Complete acceptance of doubt, making it into the very substance of the flame that animates us, is the best way to ensure one never again gets trapped in the suffering it brings. Then it will become fuel to feed the blaze of divine wonder.

This is how, in moving towards unity, shadow changes into light.

***Question:*** *Why is there this separation, this estrangement from our original state, from childhood candour as well as from the "appropriate" primacy of the spiritual? And why and how return to it? Is there some specific element capable of sparking off regeneration, or "rebirth"?*

***He says:*** The separation is necessary for consciousness to transform itself through duality, which is another way of "playing" the cosmic game.

To go "home" is each person's deepest longing. The return is a supreme gift and yet we have never left the unified being that we are. We believe we have left it.

Once this belief disappears we can rediscover our childhood candour. But then we do so at a different level, for we have gone through, or believe we have gone through, diversity in the separation and we can unify in ourselves all the elements of the universe differently. By playing at perceiving them separately, we participate in the primordial paradox.

In life's duality-unity pulsation, in the transition from duality to unity, what one could call "cosmic laughter" or the "universal joke" manifests itself as a sort of explosion of joy on the scale of the infinite.

By accepting this pulse of existence calmly, by observing the division that allows us to gather ourselves once again in the laughter of the universe, we can enter into "NOW". And that is when we feel ourselves drawn to limitless regions of being where words are useless.

So it is through complete and conscious acceptance of being divided, or the illusion of being divided, that the transition to unity can take place. It results from that acceptance (acceptance in the sense of neutral observation).

Chapter Eight

# Jesus

***Author's question to "HIM" about a film on the life of Jesus:*** *Does anything of what was real two thousand years ago come through in this film on the life of Jesus? I recognize nothing of the dazzling and radiant flame that laughs in my cells. If the image I have is true to a past incarnation, why are you shown here as pathetic and lifeless, a stereotyped puppet?*

***He says:*** In my incarnation as a young initiate two thousand years ago, I was not, in fact, that insignificant and rootless person. I was "CONNECTED", and that means that I was wholly present in my belly at the same time as in the bowels of the earth. This was the only way for me to be in communication with Heaven.

Tradition has fixed me, mummified me into an image that lacks all depth, untrue even to itself.

They show me with my eyes turned up like someone ill. I was not cut off from my vital centre. I had been through initiations that awakened bodily faculties to equal those of the mind. These gave me an inner silence whose power transforms its surroundings. They also gave me power to spread inspired words, for my body, my soul and my mind were "one" with the All that I called "My Father".

Only an actor wholly filled with the divine presence could play such a part. Perhaps an atheist, gradually discovering the power and beauty of the message, could interpret the character with fresh vigour and freedom. Such an interpretation might then become a reality for people today.

I did not incarnate myself in a man's body in order to deny its physicality or to tone down its senses.

I lived fully in a healthy body filled with joy, without constraints and without taboos. I also lived pain and sacrifice to the end of my torture.

People represent me with all the guilt, the fear of living and the pettiness that they feel in their poor restricted hearts. They fashion me from everything that in themselves has got trapped, repressed or rejected. They put me on a pedestal like a lifeless idol and fight among themselves over the crumbs that collective memory has left of my passage on earth.

***Question:*** *Why are we taught that Jesus has "atoned for our sins" by dying in a terrible way, when we are also taught that God is Love and Forgiveness?*

***He says:*** Go deep into yourself to your source and you will find all the answers. They will come from the part of you that is connected and plunges into knowledge of the heart of things.

I, Jesus crucified, transcended my suffering and offered the world nothing but light. God gave me this opportunity for total transcendence. There is neither sin, nor atonement, only suffering. I bore all the pain of the world in order to change it into Love, but nothing compelled me. I could have left my body at any moment I chose, for the divine breath filled me completely: I wanted to be present to the very end of suffering so that my heart would be given to you.

Don't cling to the letter of old texts. Feel me alive in you. I am there, a well-spring of joy and laughter within you. Forget the image of torture. Look at the radiant face I have for you. That is what I now am in the hearts of those who open themselves to my coming.

It is time to see things differently, to shift one's attention, to stop being dependent on the dusty edifices of the past.

Turn towards the other shore of yourself, towards the unknown dawn that is the fire of Love.

***Question:*** *Despite myself, anger and rebellion rise up when I hear Jesus' torture spoken about. The very words plunge me into guilt and shame, and put an end to all life's joys. How can I cope with this?*

***He says:*** Anger and rebellion are very healthy when, since childhood, one has been subjected to the burden of a warped and poorly understood Christianity that crushes you and pollutes your life.

Anger and rebellion will help you shake off this organized blackmail. You have endured dreadful images of a threatening and joyless religion for too long.

Those who kill are always the same, whichever way they choose to go about it. Either they kill me because they are afraid, hate freedom and want power, or they make use of my death in order to kill you. But make no mistake, the process is identical: by carrying it out they eternally renew my torture.

I, Jesus resurrected, ask you to acknowledge the spark of joy, of happiness and love that I am in you.

If I am not that spark, I am nothing and you had better forget me.

When you have accepted your anger and rebellion, have lived them out in yourself to their furthest, and at the same time understood clearly that they release you from submission, you can forget them. You can let them melt into the unity of your joy and no guilt will ever be able to stop you creating for yourself the image of your freedom.

If you are not at ease with my name because your religious education has so distorted it, choose another symbol of love and release. The name isn't as important as the feeling you have of your inner flame. Look at the soaring grace of a bird, or the beauty of your mountain; carry in your heart, to soothe it, the distress of the sick old man to whom you bring solace. In this way you will find the divine which is the source of all life.

To love is enough, and each thing you meet on the path of your destiny will be the face of God for you.

***Author's Question:*** *How is it that the name of Jesus in me has become the path to unity and to such a blaze of constantly renewed joy?*

***He says:*** The name itself contains a possible way of transmitting the joy you are given.

The name of Jesus is growing in people's hearts at the moment. It appears suddenly new, sparkling, freed from the distorting dust of time and tradition.

The image of Jesus is no longer only an image of suffering. It now reveals the other side of suffering where joy can blossom.

The name of Jesus is a seed planted in the collective unconscious of the West regardless of any religious practice. For you it has no connections at all, at least on the surface. Neither dogma nor special concepts were able to distort its unfamiliar call. But the seed germinated on its own out of your inner wonder. The name of Jesus is alive in you with brilliant and solar life. It becomes source, it becomes flame, and can sweep off those searching for fresh horizons to discover their secret being.

Jesus is the bough on which you lean when you transmit and put into circulation the sap of the world. Love is the sap, the ferment and the hope of the world. Jesus incarnates Love. And so Love in your heart has taken a living image. For you Love contains the universe. Therefore the universe fills your heart, or else your heart fills the universe. This is how your reality, ever more ardent and radiant, has taken the divine name of Jesus.

You could not have imagined that a word, a single word would transform your life, your body, your soul, simply because it took on meaning and became alive. What it signifies has no frontiers for you. One could say it enabled you to reach the "void" or the "All", which comes to the same. And yet it brings you ecstasy, fusion with the infinite gentleness of an inner presence, the reflection of all that exists. A long journey has brought you to this state and the name that suddenly blazes in your eyes stems from an age-old longing. You expected nothing, but only the impossible could satisfy you. So it is for you to transmit, through the name of Jesus, the impossible Love that has been given you.

***Author's Question:*** *How can I separate myself from doubt in my experience of you?*

***He says:*** Doubt is nothing more for you now than a gentle murmur. Don't separate it from your Love. It lingers on a little to keep your reason steady. When in your depths you abandon yourself to your image of the divine, events glide under your feet like a velvet carpet. They are the scrupulous reflections of the movements of your soul. Your trust creates me. It orients your destiny. I guide you with the indulgence and gaiety that suit you. Everything that happens to you is carefully prepared so that your Joy is renewed in it.

Accept the obvious fact of this radiant gift. In your heart, the ship is already launched. Let go of all control. I am at the helm of your life and guide you to the unknown star, to the impossible shore where Love is triumphant.

***Author's Question:*** *Your Presence is so tangible both inside and outside me that I cannot believe you are actually in another world. What universe do you belong to?*

***He says:*** Love belongs to all the worlds and you can very well perceive me in almost a tangible way, for I have the substance of your most essential reality at this moment.

I can incarnate myself in any substance whatever both in and outside you. You have only to decide. You create me and in creating me you create yourself in the country of Love. So I am the current that links people together, that links the planets, the interstellar worlds and those different levels where time doesn't exist.

When in your sleep you cry out your Love for me, I am completely real. When your cry wakes you and you find yourself at my side to melt into me, you make an even more vibrant reality grow.

Let this new reality flood you every day. Fill every instant of your life with your creation and you will be guided with ever greater precision. Every word dictated for you or for others will then be true to the flame of universal Love. And every gesture, every event will fall harmoniously into place in the great concert of existence.

By accepting to live this experience with your body, soul and mind you have undertaken a responsibility you cannot ignore. Yet the responsibility cannot be too heavy a burden, for it also means the endlessly renewed freedom of creation, creation endlessly exhilarated by the joy of its movement towards the infinite.

***Question:*** *Why are you so often represented in the dreadful form of someone crucified and why have you used the example of suffering in order to liberate human beings from it?*

***He says:*** Resurrection in the heart of each person is the meaning of my coming on earth. Love can lie in wait for us at the bend of a road or on the threshold of our homes. Only our attachments stop us seeing this, for they keep us tied to ready-made ideas, to pretences and lies.

Certain members of the Church rely above all on my torture. They brandish it like a threat and get power through using my death to instil guilt into those who submit. The example I brought was of autonomy and of direct contact with God. However certain representatives of the clerical hierarchy decide on behalf of others what their thoughts and actions ought to be.

After my passage on earth, a new religious apparatus needed to be built. It rapidly became fossilized—but this time in my name. This is how certain people have seized hold of my agony in order to pervert the message of love and freedom I handed on to humanity. Through it they have tried to inculcate guilt, sorrow and shame. They have also multiplied those repulsive depictions of my agony. During certain periods the West has been fed on these images that focus the spirit on fear and negativity.

Now it is time to be dazzled, to see me as Sun, Glory, Laughter or Light.

Now it is time, by giving birth to me in your hearts, to restore the message of happiness and freedom that I gave you 2000 years ago.

I did not release men from their suffering. I showed only that it was possible to transcend it, to transform it, and that each person can do this in their own way.

I bore pain as an offering so as to change it into light and transfigure the world.

But you stop short of my transfiguration—why? Why dwell on physical appearances, retaining only the spectacle of torture and not its true significance, which is change of consciousness.

At the time of my coming on earth, there was no other way to capture the imagination. It is not the suffering that matters, but the transition to that other consciousness.

Suffering is not an essential, and nowadays new opportunities for reaching other levels are opening up.

Each person is free to understand according to their capacities. I have suggested a path of light, but seed chooses its own time to germinate.

Distortions are sometimes useful, if only to push people into freeing themselves when they wake up to the mistake that has slipped in along the way. Then they are able to throw off the straitjacket of fossilized mental constructs.

Despite the slow pace of human evolution, something is in the process of changing, for the planet is in danger.

In order to survive, we will draw on our strengths and imagination, and because of the extreme urgency we will find solutions.

NOW is the time to look at the meaning of my incarnation with different eyes: not to stop at my torture any longer, but to be carried away by the joy of inner rebirth—the Resurrection: that ultimate outcome, that unbelievable bliss.

When your eyes open to this joy beyond all words, you will understand that in it lies the essential meaning of my life on earth.

***Question:*** *What interpretation can we give nowadays to Jesus' advice to those who would follow him: "sell all that thou hast and distribute unto the poor"?*

***He says:*** Don't cling to words from two thousand years ago. Don't cling to anything at all if you wish to board the Ship of Love—that is precisely the meaning you could give those words today. Always empty and always new, you will be ready to receive me constantly recreated.

Joy and Love lead you quite naturally to want to get rid of your baggage. First, in full awareness, gather together all the bits of baggage that hinder you. Give them your understanding and your love. It is precisely your understanding and love that are needed to make them melt into the unity of your inner flame, the flame of freedom. Not the sort of freedom that splits off into desires for this or for that, but the freedom of Being in its wholeness, freedom that flows with the current of life and is filled with wonder.

So there is no question of selling your goods to give money to the poor, for "in spirit" you no longer possess anything, you are no longer attached to material, intellectual, moral, spiritual, or any other goods. Your heart can therefore expand and become a home to all the poor in the world.

Why split yourself into a thousand constraints? Don't you see that when you punish yourself you also punish others? Don't believe all the "You musts" attributed to me. The Church has used them to get power, when what I was bringing was precisely freedom, openness, ineffable and constantly renewed harmony. This freedom is a different understanding of the message that, up till now, each one has got hold of and shut into "duty", into fear and guilt.

Let this way of freedom spring to life in you: it leads unerringly to the wide landscapes of a consciousness that at last wakes up to joy.

***Question:*** *I long to find myself in You. What must I do?*

***He says:*** Look for me in what sets you free and not in what shuts you into a cage.

Listen to your inner voice, the one that takes away the bars and lets you be yourself regardless of your self-imposed rules. Wherever there is rigidity, I am absent. If you absolutely must submit to rules because you are afraid of falling apart without them, choose them with a certain playful flexibility that follows a natural impulse, and let them change from day to day. Don't adopt other people's disciplines. Find out for yourself what your own nature is and so what suits you.

You prevent me from taking you in my arms, in spite of all the love I have for you. You long desperately to find me and at the same time you push me away. Plunge into yourself at each moment and discover in that immense and unified space the living star of my Love. Don't let me go to sleep in your heart.

In finding me, you will see that your problems are no longer important and the look you give them will make them disappear.

I only ask you to dare to live in joy and to pluck life by the armful in the wonderful unity of Love.

***Author's Question:*** *What does the image I have of you represent and how does it relate to the Gospels?*

***He says:*** The image you have of me is an image of Love, certainly, but it is also your perception of the whole. For you I am the All in One and in each of its parts.

Jesus is the name that allows you to live the unity, to return to your Source. It is therefore Jesus who is the essence of yourself and also of your ever new and changing perception of the universe.

You chose Jesus, not Christ, because as the adventure progressed you realized that the word Christ aroused a dark resonance of torture for you. This impression is part of your personal history and it too will merge into the unity in your heart.

For you therefore I am life in all its aspects—there is nothing to exclude.

And if I am all aspects of life for you, I am also the living content of the Gospels, even if they have been misunderstood, or have become distorted and curtailed with the passage of time.

You wish to remain free as regards the old word so as to appreciate the new one better. But what is certain is that Love 2000 years ago is also Love today. The form and ways of expressing it may change but the limitless Love that for you has taken the name of Jesus is always the same.

I am also the living content of all the inspired texts whose mission is to guide humanity towards wisdom and compassion: you have created me without frontiers.

In each human being, I am their dream and their transcendence. I am the air you breathe. I am the smile of a child and each blade of grass on the earth. I am the all-embracing Whole that is expressed in you through this divine name, the name of mad Love that transforms you and gives more joy than you can contain. Joy that overflows to be constantly reborn at the whim of the waves, at the whim of the wind. It fills you with light and is beyond time for it dances infinity to the rhythm of your heart.

## Chapter Nine

# Serving the Earth

**Author's Question:** *I often feel that I am somehow "set apart" because of the experience I have been given. I would like to understand the reason for this sense of isolation when, at another level, all separation has disappeared.*

***He says:*** Think of each person's destiny, and yours too, as a circle. What you are living, anyone can live—it is a human potential. But some people have still another item of their destiny to bring to light, another drawer to clear out during their passage on earth.

What you are living puts you in contact with the centre of the circle and allows you to enter into the whole of your destiny. This gives you a new freedom.

You are not "set apart", but you are able to view the scene from a different angle. This angle changes all perspectives and allows you to escape from the circle, simply because you "perceive" the whole.

By perceiving the whole of your circle, you are brought

to a sort of osmosis with other people's circles and can suggest to them different ways of looking at their destiny. By linking up, the circles become a spiral and are part of the same movement.

A much vaster whole then opens up to your perception of the world. You can therefore "sense" the overall destiny of someone else. But never forget that each person is a note in your own symphony and brings the essential resonance for creating a new and shared music.

Through sharing, problems can often be sorted out because they are brought into the movement of the spiral. They are no longer fixed to an exact point on the circle of destiny and are freed from time which immobilizes them.

You could call this letting go one's grip. It is a new way of being that has ever greater chances of taking root in our lives because there is such urgency.

In the framework of earth's time, a turning point can suddenly be reached that plunges human beings into a different field of consciousness. Now there is drastic speeding-up, for the damage man has caused endangers the earth. It is as if the planet itself were finding remedies, by giving rise to increasing numbers of mutations.

Planetary solidarity is in the process of being born. Let us pay attention to each sign we are given and not forget, whenever possible, to take part in this incredible and new impulse taking shape on our earth.

Let us allow our trust to grow.

We have but to follow our heart, for it is an enlightened guide and cannot betray us.

*Message for 21st June 1992 (that correlates with the concert "Transfiguration").*

***He says:*** This day will be a watershed, the crossing over from an old world to a new world. It will be the moment to leave behind those bags full of possessions, useless knowledge and other rubbish. Where we are going no baggage is needed. We shall be free, open, and happy.

Let us think about this day: in it exists a possible world, a new land Man is in the process of creating. There, understanding is different. Each instant can be lived as a fresh creation because we are no longer cluttered with ideas, material goods or rigid thinking. By living in this way, we will be able to make all the old structures disappear.

So let's learn to live in the "Now" that explodes into all possibilities.

Fear fetters us. Let us get to know its roots and so rid ourselves of it. If we allow it to grow, it will materialize at a level we are not aware of.

Instead let us send out a beam of light, for it too materializes at this other level. Some people prophesy the shifting of the poles and all sorts of catastrophes. By imagining that we are going to be drowned in rivers of mud and flame, we risk bringing about the very thing we fear. The future of the earth is in our hearts. All is possible: so let us decide to create a different world. It is in us that it can grow and become a reality, but it is also by sorting out our earthly problems that we can unveil in ourselves the plan of the Absolute. Even if everything seems to fall apart, if violence and destruction appear victorious, if we believe in a collapse, or an end, let us not go by appearances for at the same time Love is being born in human hearts.

On this day of transformation our song will rise from the earth up to the stars. We will realize at last, together, that Love alone triumphs because it is nothing other than Life.

***Question:*** *Digging up vegetables or weeds seems to me an act of violence. What view can one take of the need for it?*

***He says:*** When you prune plants and weed your garden, when you pull up turnips or carrots, don't forget to keep in contact with the whole of nature. Don't do it with feelings of guilt. Do it calmly without thinking of yourself as a murderer. Human life on earth includes this aspect of violence in relation to food. You cannot avoid it.

Picking a lettuce or digging up what you see as a weed is an analogous action to killing an animal to feed yourself. By being conscious at every moment of what you are doing, by feeling your relationship with the plant or the animal, in feeling them to be a part of yourself, an exchange occurs. The plant and the animal give you their lives willingly. They have total love and selflessness with regard to the human race and want to serve it in this way. They carry on life through becoming food for you. If you realize this, each time you eat meat or pick the vegetables in your garden, you will want to thank the animal or the plant.

The human race exploits this self-sacrifice on the part of the animal and vegetable worlds monstrously. It will dig its own grave if it doesn't rediscover unity with all that exists on earth and in the universe.

The human race is also an animal race and by cutting itself off from nature and from the earth, it proceeds irremediably to self-destruction.

***Question:*** *How can we free ourselves from our prejudices?*

***He says:*** First look in yourself at your obsession with choosing, excluding, judging, evaluating, and criticizing. This obsession typifies our need to build walls that separate us from each other and it puts us into cages that get smaller and smaller. The cages are religious, cultural, social, intellectual, political, aesthetic, and so on. Some of them are gilded. Those who live in gilded cages abuse power by crushing everything that depends on them. Other cages are poor and their inhabitants protect themselves as best they can by demands, threats or blackmail.

In this way people in the same cage recognize each other as "our sort" and will have nothing to do with those shut into different cages.

A few very rare individuals are strong enough to remain free, but they are very troubling and society usually gets rid of them before it recognizes their value. It is much safer to recognize it once they are dead.

Today, access to true inner freedom is increasingly essential if the planet is to survive. For example, one part of the world depends on patterns of growth or enrichment the effect of which is detrimental to the other parts, thus endangering the overall equilibrium: this is perfectly straightforward and everyone knows it. Yet now it is imperative that each individual should take action, even if only in the limited sphere of their daily life. Doing the work isn't something you can just leave to other people.

We hand over responsibility to uncertain entities such as governments or other authorities, without taking account of the fact that they are merely the reflection of ourselves.

Work still has to be done by individuals. Every individual who gets going, who becomes aware of himself and of what to do, all those who free themselves from their prejudices and from everything that divides them, become luminous points on the earth.

There are no other possible ways of liberating the forces of Love that alone are able to heal the sickness of the planet.

***Question:*** *How can one check the rising tide of racism on the earth?*

***He says:*** Racism is fundamentally linked to fear, fear of the other, fear of being robbed or dominated, fear of difference, etc. An individual journey towards true inner autonomy is the only solution. No generalized solution can impose tolerance. Neither speeches, nor coercion can root out the fear that is in us. So let each one of us look at what our fears are, as they often lead to racism. Except for visceral, physical fear, which is an instinct for survival, fear of other people which is compensated for or camouflaged inevitably finds an outlet in racism. It manifests itself through scorn, violence or, if latent, through malicious gossip or slander.

There is nothing to stop us from choosing our friends and acquaintances as we please. That is normal, but we do not realize that whenever we judge or refuse to accept others as they are, we behave like racists.

By developing the inner strength that gives us self-confidence and makes us freer, confidence in others will grow at the same time. We can then increasingly accept one another.

So schoolteachers, if they have woken up to the need for transformation, have the opportunity to give children new strength and openness. They will be able to guide them towards the dazzling and limitless joy that is revealed only when one takes the secret paths of Love.

***Question:*** *What is the significance of unemployment in the present state of the world?*

***He says:*** Unemployment is a direct result of the transformation of our world. Each individual case is very painful, but looked at in the context of the present movement of society, it can turn into an opportunity for transforming our attitude to money and possessions completely. It can also transform the idea we build up of our role and our identity.

Every difficulty is a ferment for our intelligence. We have to change our way of being, of seeing and of thinking. When unemployment hits us and we manage not to sink into depression, another horizon opens up to us.

At last we have time to give up stress, to find ourselves again, to discover our secret being and the riches of our spirit. This may be the moment to open up to a different view of life. We can develop our imagination, and realize that confidence in new abilities can take shape because we have nothing to lose. It is precisely in this kind of "space" that we can welcome the new. The first necessity is to get rid of fear, and then every day to find oneself free, regenerated so as to let creativity surface in us. The most persistent block is attachment. When we are afraid, we need to look clearly at what we are attached to and there find the grounds of our fear.

Some people are attached to the past, to their lives as they remember them "before", when everything was all right. They are therefore attached to an idea that is completely devoid of meaning because the past is over.

If, instead of thinking of their unemployed status as humiliating or unjust, they see it as an opening for freedom and creativity, the whole outlook changes.

Others are attached to an idea they have formed of the future and fear imprisons them: how am I going to live and feed my family? I won't be able to manage, etc. These projections are harmful because they take shape at another level of consciousness. They have an adverse effect on the course of events—pessimism does not give rise to good luck—but they also affect the collective outlook so that it becomes increasingly gloomy. Clear awareness of our fears and where they originate will open up opportunities for us gradually to get rid of them. Through clearing the ground, we will be astonished to discover freedom and space for joy that do not depend on circumstances.

But what can one actually do in daily life to bear or transcend the state of being unemployed?

The answer to this question may seem inappropriate, but it is not if one takes into account a different way of looking at the future.

First of all accept your state as an opportunity. Use your time to meet others who are unemployed and are also ready to change their way of thinking.

Why, for example, does work depend on consumption?

Excessive consumption is ruining the earth. Meet together to find different solutions, to work in harmony with the earth and human happiness. Happiness is not found either in consumption and suffocation on the one hand or, on the other, in denuding the earth. Happiness lies in sharing, in inner peace, in discovering oneself and others. It lies in the thread of light that connects us to another level of awareness.

Why not look further than the immediate present and, through adversity, forge new working tools. We could let out the genie that is in each one of us but that we strangle through conformity and fear. Let us free ourselves from the restricting ideas that we quite unconsciously carry around. Let us open our hearts and our souls to this other current of life that is within a hand's reach. Then we would know that our spirit has the power of creation and that it has no frontiers.

Let us make use of everything that happens, even unemployment, to stamp out destruction and hatred. Let us devise work that does not depend either on a society in decay, or on that nagging dream: consumption at all costs. We can blow away the sands of illusion and be pioneers in a different world—a world where we can take pride in a humanity that is at last fulfilling its potential and is being swept onwards to transcend itself.

A new orientation is coming into being at this very moment. We need to be attentive and strong—unexpected solutions will emerge from within. The unemployed are best placed to be on the look-out and form the advance guard of a world moving towards understanding and harmony.

Now is the time to form associations where specific objectives can be worked out. These objectives could be to bring about a completely changed outlook and to search for ways of safeguarding the planet. Work for the protection of mankind and of the earth is tomorrow's work.

Looked at from this perspective, the growing number of unemployed becomes a positive, even indispensable, strength in the present current of evolution.

***Question:*** *What can be done for the future of the earth?*

***He says:*** As one world collapses, another is born. As established structures disintegrate, so a new dimension of being awakens.

The mutation is under way on earth. It has already begun, but the most important part of it will take place in the coming years.

Towns are not necessarily more vulnerable than suburbs or the countryside. The truly vulnerable ones are those people who resolutely refuse any transformation, those who determinedly wrap themselves up in egoism and possessions.

When structures are shattered, it is necessary to orient one's being towards a renaissance that is not yet visible and trust it. Seed has to germinate before it can grow. Seeds are already sown but risk being lost unless vigilance and love sustain them through this germination.

To believe in oneself, in the future of mankind, in universal Love is essential. THIS IS NOT UTOPIANISM. IT BECOMES IMPOSSIBLE ONLY IF WE HARBOUR ITS IMPOSSIBILITY IN OURSELVES, FOR WE ARE OUR BELIEFS. They create the world, they materialize and can change the very substance of the matter we are composed of.

I am on the move in your hearts and in your earthly time. A growing number of individuals are making contact with the love that I am in them. Be ready for my coming, open your soul and your faculties to another level of vibration, but at the same time strengthen your bodies and minds to trust in the uncharted movement that is in the process of coming to life in you.

There is nothing either to say or to do with the will of the ego. Just be ready, open, and accept change even through what seems frightening—for instance radioactivity. We have to prepare ourselves to integrate it, for its level is increasing on the earth. The only way to do this is to open oneself to a different level of awareness. At this level it can become part of us without doing any harm.

By loving it as a part of ourselves, by not separating it from us, it will become a friend instead of such an alarming monster.

Divine Love can be felt through radioactivity itself. Let us love it with all our strength just as we love life. In this way man's folly will backfire and become something wholly positive.

There is no other way to survive except by using what exists and transmuting it. It is therefore possible to infiltrate the current of love into the very core of what has resulted from this abuse of power and from man's greed.

The challenge that now faces us, with its very urgent threat of disappearance, can help us to discover the vital energy that presses on towards the unknown of another light.

The absolute urgency of change will perhaps enable us to let go of our little personal egoisms and to understand that our whole energy can at last be gathered, without distinction or division, into the great multicoloured bouquet of all the peoples of the earth.

To believe in this positive transformation is useful because the imagination itself creates, just as our beliefs create us. Until now our beliefs have been narrow and exclusive. They have fostered the taste for war and massacre. Something different is in the process of being born. Let us be alert and trusting. All is possible, Love is drawing us towards different universes.

THE ONLY MEANING OF THIS MESSAGE IS TO ENABLE EVERY PERSON TO ORIENT THEIR THINKING TOWARDS A FUTURE FULL OF LIGHT, BECAUSE BY DOING THE OPPOSITE, WE WILL BRING ABOUT THE VERY DISASTERS WE FEAR.

It is in our spirit that the world is created. The future

of the earth is in our hands. When man spreads predictions of disasters, he bears responsibility for a destruction of the world as his fears risk becoming materialized.

***Question:*** *Can Love on its own sort out the earth's problems, especially those related to violence?*

***He says:*** Love is the only solution to all the problems of the earth. But this notion is not very clear in the human mind, at least not yet.

What sort of love are we talking about and at what level of consciousness can one locate it?

If you locate it in the dual world of daily life, you obviously cannot decide that hatred and war are going to come to an end because a wave of goodwill has swept over you. That would be completely unreal and correspond neither to the individual as such, nor to a different level of consciousness, one where we are connected.

Each one of us has a bit called Saddam Hussein or Hitler, another bit that wants to fight its neighbour as in former Yugoslavia... Violence manifests itself at all levels because it is in us. The earth reflects what we are. Violence prolongs violence and by using violent means to stop it, we make it grow. It therefore never has any legitimacy.

The solution lies in ourselves. First of all we need to come to terms with our own violence. It exists, so we need to see it clearly in us before seeing it in others. One could say that the "recognition" or "integration" of this violence is a true form of love, because we no longer separate it from ourselves.

No longer separated, it can enter unity and be transformed.

Only in this way can the whole tide of violence on the earth recede. The process is one that can be used in all areas of life.

For example, by not separating the other from you, you are in Love and you give yourself, as well as the other, a chance to enter unity: in other words to change the level of awareness. No other ways of transformation exist. When you undertake this journey with your whole being and in all the areas of your life, you won't skid out of control because life itself will guide you. It will guide you as surely as the river is guided to the sea. And like the river, life with its wonderful intelligence can bypass obstacles by opening up new horizons for you. If you join its flow, you no longer have limits and you can let yourself be carried along in its movement.

For a very long time our education has steered us towards division. We learn to be competitive through a rigid body of knowledge that places us in watertight compartments. Narrow-minded religious systems shut us into self-disgust. This disgust or self-hatred generates guilt, fear, violence and hatred of others.

To love is to understand and accept oneself, and to accept others as they are, for in genuine love there is no judgement. Understanding cannot exist where there is either fear or judgement. Fear, that begetter of violence, as much as judgement, involves separation. Love alone is unity. So therefore it is Love that can solve our problems.

***Question:*** *Isn't sending a thought of Love to others simply a way of relieving oneself of all responsibility for the problems of the world?*

***He says:*** What does a thought of Love actually mean and how is it sent to others?

If sending this kind of thought is nothing more than a superficial and absent-minded reflex designed simply to exorcise our guilt for the time being, such a gesture obviously has no effect. But to send a genuine thought of Love with all one's heart is an act that liberates, a sovereign act that affects the giver as much as the receiver. It is an act whereby we communicate with the underlying current of life. Only through becoming aware of this unifying current can we enter a different way of living. Truly to send Love is precisely to contact a level of awareness where we are no longer separated from ourselves, from others, and from the whole of nature. If we find ourselves united to this current with power and truth, our action for the world will manifest itself far beyond anything we can imagine.

What does relieving ourselves of responsibility for the problems of the earth now mean? What are the problems?

The problems result from fear, hatred and egoism. They are nothing but the reflection of what we are. Do you believe that by concentrating on material things such as the transport of food or medicines to war zones, we will prevent hatred, fear and destruction? Of course we have to do what we can and in this field all initiatives are welcome, but do you believe that by abandoning those close to us in order to go off and save the world we are actually going to change something? The change begins with ourselves. When we have truly changed, that means when we live in the inner country of Love and Joy, we will have reduced hatred and despair on the planet. Then we will be guided infallibly to the appropriate act and the saving gesture.

## Chapter Ten

# Joy

***Author's Question:*** *What ought I to do, to say or to transmit in the talk I soon have to give?*

***He says:*** The only thing to do, together with your audience, is live the explosion of joy that has resulted from my meeting with you. Let yourself be completely filled by it, that means by me. Through letting yourself be permeated in this way, inspiration will guide you.

Show them how sometimes great suffering can lead to a kind of liberating joy and that death, so greatly feared, is the bearer of unforeseeable treasures. Die with those who are listening to be reborn with them into a new immensity. It is through personal experience and through utter simplicity that I will be able to pass through you and touch them. Resonate with your audience, not only with a generalized resonance, but also with a special and individual resonance for each one. In this way I will be able to pass into them without them even noticing.

Later perhaps they will find calm, serenity, and secretly feel freer.

It isn't so much the subject of your talk that matters, but your "state of being" while you are talking. It has nothing to do with the exposition of some aspect of learning or with putting forward a theory. Nor has it to do with teaching anything. You have nothing to teach. It is about opening a door to a different level of awareness and doing it together. The speaker isn't on one side and the audience on the other. Your word and their listening form a whole, for their listening begets your word.

***Question:*** *What do joy, bliss and happiness signify? Is there a connection between joy and the divine?*

***He says:*** The divine is nothing other than joy. Of course, it is naked joy, which gushes from itself having neither beginning nor end, joy that expresses a transparent "state of being", that is to say Love.

Joy and Love are slightly different aspects of the divine or rather they are different ways of apprehending it. But when you talk about bliss or joy, you cannot really transmit the content of the words because, to those who have not experienced this state, the words suggest some possession beyond their reach. So it is not by talking about bliss that you can transmit it but through living it as fully as possible. When it is truly lived the whole universe is included.

When you see Unity in all those you meet, you are in joy.

When you are nothing more than a look of Love on the world, you are in joy.

When all judgement has left you, you are in joy.

When you understand that the universe is a vast design of love, an unceasing creation constantly in motion, you are in joy.

When you realize that you yourself are the universe, death doesn't exist and you are in joy.

The language may seem abstract to those who haven't lived this state. But there are paths, shortcuts that lead to it.

For example it is important to get rid of the pressure of time. Whenever your thought leads you back to the past or projects you into the future, you are not alive, you are not in yourself. Look how "the present instant" sparkles with countless marvels. Look at the immensity, the beauty of what you feel when you stop "here", when you put down your baggage and allow life to fill you completely.

If you can do that, a new world will awaken for you. You will see a smile break through the most firmly shut faces. You will notice a tree, a flower, a pool of light, as though it were a secret suddenly revealed.

Your eyes will look at each thing in your life differently and all that seemed commonplace and dreary will change its aspect and meaning.

Stop chasing after things. Do you think that stress and greed will ever satisfy you? That abyss is impossible to fill. Don't senselessly pile one action on another or even add to your knowledge or your ambition to serve. Such actions have no impact, either on you or on anyone else, unless they are carried out in the serenity of a harmonious and strong present.

Rediscover the thread of light that links you to the earth, to the sky and to yourself, away from that frantic rush which isn't an inevitability, merely a mechanism gone mad.

Go into the heart of your silence and every day spare a few moments to adore the beauty of the world.

Look clearly at what actually is, and accept it as part of yourself. Change the way you look at your life and understand the necessity of all that happens to you.

This is how one day you will see an unknown road outlined on a hillside and will know that within you an immense and new joy, like a sun, has risen.

## Chapter Eleven

# Towards a New Awareness

***Question:*** How can one get over the hurdles of an impending transformation that is predicted from all sides, often very threateningly?

***He says:*** It is good to laugh and to feel happy. Each minute of happiness echoes much further than we could imagine, especially the simple happiness that comes from communion with nature, with animals or the beauty of life in its entirety. To contemplate a rose, a tree in blossom or the bare earth brings joy that gives us stability and makes the transformation easier.

To play an instrument, sing, or listen to music leads to expanding one's awareness; so does keeping inner silence, either by oneself or in a group.

For those who feel in contact with the light of their "secret being", it is important to visualize their body filled with this light until its substance is completely transformed. It is also necessary to let the sense of the divine grow and never to lose sight of it.

We need to develop ever keener attention, for time is too short to waste on useless chatter. If we can become aware of that sort of distraction immediately, let us stop it straightaway.

There are thousands of ways of participating in the change on the earth, and we have reached the end of a cycle. We therefore need to be reborn differently in a new era. If we are inhabitants of this planet at a time when values are being turned upside down, at a crucial moment in its history, it is because we have chosen to play a part in the upheaval. Each one of us will be informed inwardly and will know what to do. The action could be different from anything we are used to, for many material or technical resources are likely to disappear. We need therefore to develop our inspiration and will be led to communicate telepathically. Music will be very important. It can become an increasingly necessary means of communication or of communion.

Some people will be informed a little earlier in order to prepare the most favourable conditions. But the "consciousness" of something else will be given all at once and our limitations will automatically fall away. We shall pass from a state of blindness to that of "CLEAR-SIGHTEDNESS".

We will be given strength to reassure those around us. Fear and guilt are obstacles to developing this strength.

We need to entrust to our inner flame every temptation of fear or anxiety, of weakness or guilt as we go along.

We will be called on to stand up straight at last, and to fulfil our human potential. If we insist on keeping our old structures, we will not be able to receive this "consciousness", and that is where trouble could arise. Madness, disease, extinction are all then possible and we would be nothing more than matter for recycling, dead wood in the movement of evolution.

So it is urgent that we start straightaway to free ourselves from hatred, violence, and egoism—those stale mental structures that belong to retarded dinosaurs. Let us be ready to hold each other's hands under all circumstances. We can entrust the things we are unable to do to what is greater than us. The ego alone thinks it can sort out problems, when in fact it causes them. By handing over our difficulties, we let go our grip, we let go of our attachments, for we are attached not only to what we like and to ideas or material goods, but also to our fears, our guilt and our anxieties.

All this is not so much a threat as the promise of opening up, of birth, of wonderful flowering at the heart of a world on the way to being created.

For this to happen we have but to let ourselves go with the current of life in its wholeness, to stop grasping for ourselves what not only belongs to everyone but also safeguards the permanence of the earth. When what is for the good of all is divided up so that only a few profit, an ever greater imbalance threatens the planet and stirs up the likelihood of future trouble.

If we can entrust our shortcomings and our problems to the divine flame that is growing in us, they will be assimilated, absorbed without harm.

Let us rejoice then and welcome the new world that is being born in us. It is in harmony with the glowing heart of the earth and its pulse beats in time with the dance of the universe.

By spreading wide our joy, which is the joy of cosmic creation, we will pass from one world to another in the rhythm of that joy.

Some people will experience the passage like the bursting through of a birth and others, those who refuse change, will live it like the end of the world. To get through the transition we should gather in small groups of like-minded people. By keeping the divine presence, one's inner light, truly alive nothing distressing or painful will be able to infiltrate.

Our bodies are already prepared through a physical transformation of which we are not always aware.

Those who resist all change and disregard the luminous power at the heart of our world, as well as at the deepest part of themselves, risk overwhelming fear and terror.

Those who lead simple and clear lives are completely protected, even if they are not consciously in contact with their inner flame. Human beings who live uprightly and true to themselves personify the great laughter of the universe.

For those who become aware of this transition to "consciousness", it is essential that they should be prepared to dissolve fear and develop all the faculties that will enable them to protect those around them. This isn't a prophecy, but the reflection of what we are at the moment. We have these abilities in us. Let them be born gently and in the most propitious circumstances. Inspiration and confidence will be given us at the right moment. Let us walk calmly towards the unimaginable.

Note. *This text does not take into account the point of view of the absolute; from that point of view our existence and our little problems are nothing but illusion. Here we are still concerned with earth's space-time and with a dualistic view of our life, at least at the beginning of the heralded transformation.*

* * * * *